SIGN
SYMBOL
&
FORM

20

SIGN SYMBOL & FORM

LOUISE BOWEN BALLINGER & RAYMOND A. BALLINGER

Remaining from a slower-paced era, this aged sign of stone with incised numerals and symbolic fleur-de-lys still graces a roadside in France.

VNR VAN NOSTRAND REINHOLD COMPANY
NEW YORK CINCINNATI TORONTO LONDON MELBOURNE

To

JEAN KOEFOED

for

INSPIRATION, GUIDANCE
AND FRIENDSHIP

Van Nostrand Reinhold Company Regional Offices:
New York Cincinnati Chicago Millbrae Dallas

Van Nostrand Reinhold Company International Offices:
London Toronto Melbourne

Library of Congress Catalog Card Number 73-163314

Designed by Louise Bowen Ballinger and Raymond A. Ballinger

Type set by Cooper & Beatty, Limited

Printed and Bound by Bijutsu Shuppan-Sha, Tokyo, Japan

Published in 1972 by Van Nostrand Reinhold Company
A division of Litton Educational Publishing, Inc.
450 West 33rd Street, New York, N.Y. 10001

Published simultaneously in Canada by
Van Nostrand Reinhold Ltd.

16 15 14 13 12 11 10 9 8 7 6 5 4 3 2 1

During the preparation of the material for any book certain individuals give unusual aid and encouragement to the project. We wish to express our appreciation to Mr. Jean Koefoed of the Van Nostrand Reinhold Company for his enthusiasm and guidance and to his associates, Nancy C. Newman and Judith Vanderwall, for their assistance in editing the manuscript. A friend of many years, himself an eminent designer, Mr. Arthur Williams, has lent suggestions and encouragement. We would like especially to mention his own designs for excellent signs illustrated on page 23 (gourmet shop, left center) and on pages 95 and 166. The technical assistance of Mr. Henry J. Laverty and Mr. Thomas J. Laverty in processing enlargements of the black-and-white photography was accomplished with their usual skill and enthusiasm and is warmly appreciated. We are delighted that Jean Koefoed required that the black-and-white portion of this book be printed by the gravure process, and that he entrusted this and the color production to Mr. Atsushi Oshita of Bijutsu Shuppan-Sha in Tokyo, Japan. Although this was written before actual printing began, we were assured of the care and technical skill that has been evident in other fine books printed by this distinguished organization.

We are indebted to all of the designers and craftsmen, individuals, and organizations whose signs have been the source of inspiration for this book and the impetus for a search of many years and many miles' duration. We trust that the inclusion of their signs will be considered as the highest of compliments.

The authors acknowledge with great appreciation the use of illustrations and information from two books, *The Book of Signs* by Rudolf Koch and *Symbols, Signs and Signets* by Ernest Lehner, graciously offered and allowed by Dover Publications, Inc. of New York. These books are two from a series known as the Dover Pictorial Archives, and are recommended to artists and designers for their excellence.

CONTENTS

FOREWORD 9

1 **THE SYMBOL AND THE SIGN** 11

2 **THE FORM**
- Things — Actual Objects 25
- Symbols 31
- Flags and Pennants 52
- Human Forms 59
- The Cross 64

3 **UNCLASSIFIED FORMS** 68

4 **THE DECORATIVE SIGN** 82

5 **MATERIALS AND FABRICATION**
- Wood 94
- Iron 103
- Silver, Gold and Other Metals 111
- Paint and Picture 118
- Glass or Window 126
- Light — Plastics and Neon 134

6 **LETTERING AND NUMERALS** 140

7 **SIGNS AND ARCHITECTURE** 148

8 **TRAVEL AND DIRECTION** 170

BIBLIOGRAPHY 191

SUN
TRUST HOUSE

FOREWORD

This book came about as a collaboration between two people intensely involved in art and design. Because of this interest, a search for good graphic forms—signs and symbols—arose as a natural extension of our professional activities. Whenever and wherever we travel, cameras are slung over our shoulders against a moment when we see a sign, symbol or design of unusual interest and merit. What started as a search for signs in the expected sense of the word, was broadened unexpectedly by capturing on film signs of a peripheral nature, such as a tasteful and exciting display of wares in front of a shop or designs or letters in ceramics or metal embedded in the street under our feet. Soon the collection was comprehensive enough to help dispel the almost universal feeling that all signs are tawdry and tasteless. A book seemed the proper vehicle to show this collection.

It is impossible to set forth with a particular destination in mind to collect photographs of good signs. Though one cannot move about without being confronted by signs, it is often difficult to come upon an example which is worthy of being recorded for its good, efficient design. Certain areas do have a bigger percentage of noteworthy examples among their total signage; for instance, at recent world's fairs and in some places in Europe, concerted efforts have been made to design graphics, including total signage, with unusually high standards and a sense of significant purpose.

Any analysis of what makes a good sign is extremely difficult, since one can find signs of charm and elegance that were produced by craftsmen working in the idiom of folk art and others that were designed and constructed by the most sophisticated technicians. Although some of the most aesthetically satisfying signs have been products of other, more technologically primitive eras, on occasion one comes upon examples in contemporary materials such as metals, plastics, and neon tubing that are excellent by any standards.

The one area of this broad spectrum not included in this book is graphics from total corporate-design programs that include coordinated programs for signs and sign usage. Much has been accomplished in this area by such organizations as General Motors, International Business Machines, Westinghouse, Radio Corporation of America, Bell Telephone, and others. The excellent signs resulting from these programs often have been applauded. But such design programs are so vast and so far reaching that they deserve more space and consideration than it is possible to give them here. (See Bibliography on page 191.)

This volume may be useful to signmakers, architects, town and traffic planners, graphic designers and, of course, those actually engaged in commerce and industry who are seeking inspiration for signs for their own organizations. This book also may be of interest to those who, although not actually engaged in the arts, are, nevertheless, appreciative of the place of art and design in man's environment. We hope that signs, as we have presented them here, will be seen as a part of man's artistic heritage. In a world where competition, congestion, speed, and accidents have increasingly taken their toll, signs should soothe rather than irritate. By making signs more efficient, effective, and aesthetic, we can improve our contemporary living.

The sun and other celestial bodies often appear as symbols or signs.
This golden sun identifies a well-known insurance company in England.

ABOUT THE PHOTOGRAPHS

All of the photographs in this book, both color and black-and-white, were taken by the authors during their search for good signs, with the exception of the following. They were taken, and kindly loaned for reproduction, by friends who became enthusiastic about the project:

Page 23 — Restaurant sign — Boston
The Rev. and Mrs. F. Lee Richards

Page 58 — Mock trousers and shirt — San Pedro Sula, Honduras
Mrs. Theodore Heysham, Jr.

The seventeenth-century Italian sign on Page 31 is reproduced from a staff photograph from the Victoria and Albert Museum, London.

1 THE SYMBOL AND THE SIGN

The sun face, an almost universal symbol from time immemorial of radiance, truth, source of life, beauty, light, used on manuscripts, old inn signs, insurance company signs, banners, flags, travel folders, and numerous contemporary objects.

So closely interwoven in the long fabric of the past are signs and symbols of communication that it becomes difficult to define with clarity the difference in meaning between them. When man or beast left a footprint in a muddy swamp, it was an unplanned sign that some living being had been there; when Indians of North America bent limbs of trees in their path or arranged piles of stones, these were planned signs. On the other hand, Northwest Coast Indians used symbols, stylized bird and animal forms carved in wood and painted, to identify clan, tribal, or family groups.

The two terms, however, are often used interchangeably, and their functions combined in one graphic design. As a symbol, the well-known Rx of the druggist and physician stands for the prescription. When this symbol is used on a wooden, metal, or plastic form hanging outside the shop, it then becomes a sign of wares or services of that shop. It may aid in the understanding of this complicated division to classify a sign as a distinguishing mark or characteristic. It might be a combination or separate use of letters and forms to communicate an idea, to warn, or to explain an area's contents. It also might be a mark, a token of something intangible. On the other hand, the symbol can be classified as a form that stands for something by relationship, suggestion, interpretation, resemblance, or association. It also might be a form that reveals quantity, special elements, or varieties.

The flag of Denmark, a white cross on a red field; similar crosses can be seen on the flags of Sweden, Norway, Finland and other countries.

Much of our written means of communication today can be traced to symbols of the past. Pictographs of Indians, Eskimos, and other early groups involved symbols that were derived from simplified shapes—man, animal, tree, abode, sun, rain, lightning—which, placed in a certain order, communicated an idea or message. Chinese writing, with its infinite variety of characters, is based on traditional brush drawings of symbols representing objects of everyday life. It is interesting to note that the written characters of the word or idea *ten thousand* is a stylized form of a scorpion. Sumerian cuneiform writing involved signs or marks that sometimes signified the name of the object and sometimes were related to its phonetic aspect. In the Phoenician alphabet the first letter is pronounced *alf,* and grew out of the ancient way of using the symbol of the head of an ox, and the second letter, *bet*, relates to the old symbol of the house. Later, these became the alpha and

Facsimile of a watermark found on paper made in the eighteenth century by William Parks, Williamsburg, Virginia.

Symbol for the male bloom, the male bird, the human male, the planet Mars, and other references.

Crowns, the symbol of royalty, when used in threes, stood for the three Magi.

Botanical symbols, annual and biennial plants.

Porcelain mark, Ludwigsburg, 1806.

Mithras, the sun, the light, the truth—a Persian deity.

Mythical bird, Northwest Coast Indian family totem.

Kame, the tortoise, Japanese symbol of longevity.

Stonemason's signature of Gothic times, found on old churches.

Housemark of Michelangelo.

Imperial crest of the Empress of Japan is related to ancient textile patterns used on clothing and other belongings.

Chemical symbol for vinegar.

beta of the Greek alphabet, the source of our alphabet. Thus, our alphabet developed from these ancient signs and symbols.

Nonverbal signs and symbols have always played a vital part in the communication of ideas. Throughout the history of man, the basic needs for sustenance, warmth, shelter, protection, inspiration, and direction have been so important that means of communicating those needs have developed in a great variety of ways. House or holding marks were private identification of peasant property. They were symbols of ownership that might be painted on sacks of fleece, punched on logs floated down the river, or embroidered on rugs or cloths. Later, these were used for family symbols or crests and incorporated into trademarks of families of craftsmen or artists. Tradesmen's cards and special watermarks on paper often used the symbols that had been handed down through generations.

Botanical signs, such as a circle with one dot in the center for an annual plant and two dots for a biennial, are still in use. The ring or circle, a nearly universal form, when used with a seal becomes a symbol of authority. Five intertwining circles became the symbol of the International Olympics. The three gold balls of the pawnbroker are said to represent three bags of gold St. Nicholas tossed into the window of a house of three poor sisters who needed dowries to get husbands. A graphic derivative of the circle, the symbol of the sun, or sun face, denotes power and can be seen on early Roman seals, on coins or banners of Louis XIV—Sun King of France, on Egyptian carvings and papyrus, on Aztec carvings, and in the art of many other cultures. Old maps used astrological and astronomical symbols with wind and sun forms embodying human characteristics. Insurance company signs and old inn signs with sun faces can still be seen.

The crown was also used as a symbol of authority, and came to be placed on tavern signs, heraldic devices, and carved forms above doorways to indicate royal patronage. The symbols seen on college seals and national, state, and city flags and seals are reminders of the past. The beautiful designs of traditional Japanese family crests may still be found on urns, temples, parchments, and fabrics. The Roman ax in the fasces, a symbol of authority, can be seen on an old ten-cent piece of the United States. The symbols

The pineapple, a symbol of hospitality, is found on furniture, gateposts, and entranceways to eighteenth-century homes.

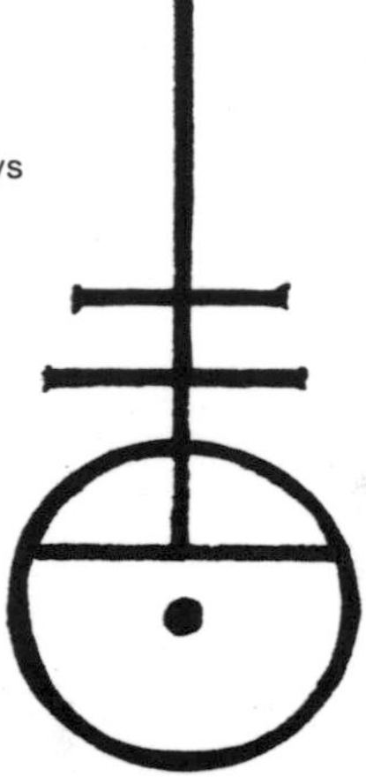

Printer's mark of the Society of Printers, Venice; many variations of this cross and orb were used in Italy in the fifteenth and sixteenth centuries.

The crown, an elegant symbol of royal or noble heritage or patronage, with its many variations of form has been much used, and continues to have great design potential.

The three fleur-de-lys were on the arms of the eleventh-century Welsh King of Gwent (Monmouthshire) and on other Welsh noble family arms. The early twelfth-century royal arms of England included the three fleur-de-lys of France, and may also be seen on decorative wrought iron, fabrics, and jewelry.

The old symbol of the sacred eye of Egypt was used on ships, manuscripts, and carvings to denote the all-seeing eye of the gods.

The Green Tree plaque is still seen on private homes and buildings, a reminder that the house was insured by the Philadelphia Contributionship for the Insurance of Houses from Loss by Fire.

An elegant natural design form, the shell has been used as a symbol on banners, coats of arms, shoulder badges, and insignia to indicate participation in a pilgrimage or crusade. It can also be seen on signs for seafood restaurants, as a symbol for a well-known oil company, and on escutcheons and furniture.

of hands or a tree, on cast iron fire marks still in use today, were placed on houses to indicate that they were insured by a specific company. In 1752, in Philadelphia, at the inspiration of Benjamin Franklin, the Philadelphia Contributionship for Insurance of Houses from Loss by Fire was founded. The tree was chosen by this company—and later by others—because the proximity of trees to a house was an important factor in determining the terms of the insurance. The eye was used as a decoration and as a symbol on Egyptian ships to ensure the vessel's safe passage and attainment of its planned destination. The shell, an almost perfect geometric design, has been used from early times, and through the ages has been associated with the goddess Venus. It was used by pilgrims and Crusaders, and is most commonly seen today as a symbol of the Shell Oil Company.

Many of today's signs and symbols originated in medieval times or in the sixteenth and seventeenth centuries. The following paragraph from Paul Zumther's *Daily Life in Rembrandt's Holland* gives a suggestion of the development of the use of symbols and signs at that time:

> Often, even the house itself took its name from the profession of its occupant. The wealthy inscribed their family name and coat of arms on the pediment above the door. The frontages of less exalted houses carried a cast-iron sign upon which was painted a realistic or allegorical design indicating the owner's trade, or at least the virtues particularly admired in that establishment: a pot for the potter, a scissors or St. Martin tearing his cloak for the tailor. People would talk of "going to the Scissors." In one particular sales contract a house was described as "the House of the Bell, in the main street opposite the Brush, near Ironmonger's Street, in Dordrecht." . . .With the rapid expansion of handicrafts and commerce during the seventeenth century, these signs multiplied. Dordrecht was famous for the number and variety of its signs. Some people commissioned well-known artists to design them ...Pastry cooks displayed pictures of St. Nicholas or St. Osbert, or simply an oven, while doctors displayed a urinal vessel. The surgeon stuck up outside his door or window a pole with a yellow tip and white, red, and blue stripes; of the em-

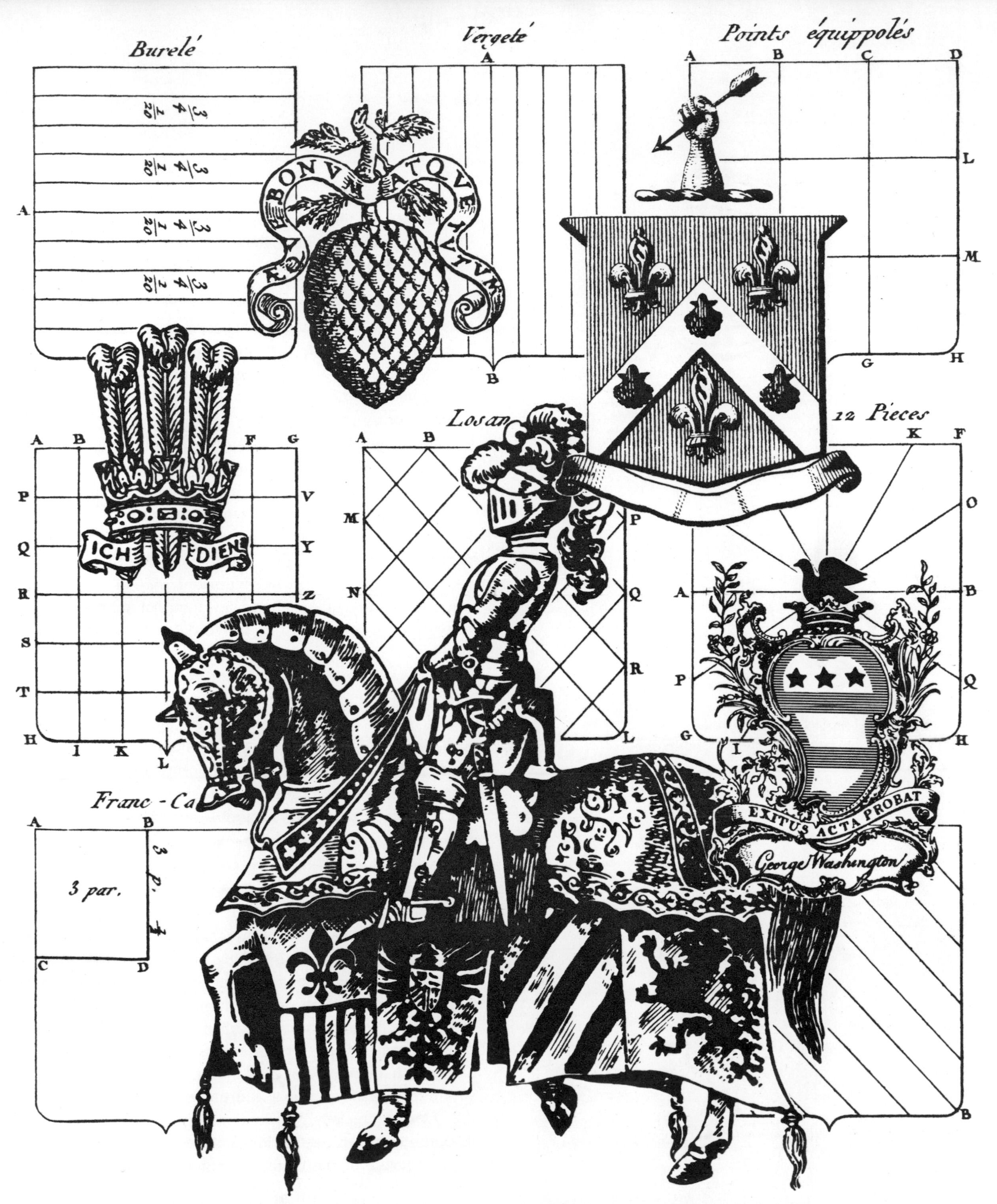

Clockwise: a French knight of the sixteenth century with symbols on his horse explaining the knight's identity as well as his status; three feathers of the Prince of Wales known as the Ostrich Feathers Badge, particular ensign of the heir apparent, bearing the motto, *Ich Dien* ("I serve") below the coronet; printer's mark with a pine cone, Giacomo Vicenzi, Venezia, 1589; arms including shells, indicating that an ancestor, perhaps, had been on a crusade to Spain or the Holy Land, H. Johnson, Esq., England; coat of arms of George Washington including the stars and bars later incorporated into the flag of the United States.

blematic colors, the white signified that here one could get teeth pulled and fractures treated, the red that one could undergo bleeding and the blue that one could get a shave.[1]

As the population of many areas and countries expanded, clear, effective, and often beautiful signs developed. There are many instances where old signs have been retained, indicating a continuity of ownership or at least an impression of stability of the business or services offered. Contemporary as well as older signs that relate to articles within the shop become a fascinating study. In many European countries one sees signs indicating by their symbols that keys are made, wine is sold, food is served, and so on. The sign may relate to the form of the structure, identify the building, or state the services rendered. It may be posted on a kiosk to give information regarding coming events. A sign may be an important part of a roadway, warning of difficulties ahead for motorist or pedestrian: heavy traffic, deer crossing, traffic lights at the next intersection, or dangerous curve. Highway signs often employ graphic symbols that can be interpreted quickly in a more effective way than words: a red flash symbolizes danger and a dotted or continuous line on the highway, safety when passing. In the same way, the language of nautical flags gives quick interchange of information or warning of storms or hurricanes brewing at sea.

As a part of a sign, the symbol is often strong and direct. Religious symbols such as the star, the cross, the seven-branch candlestick, the dove, and others from the past are widely used. The coffee cups above a cafe give an obvious suggestion of a coffee break. The well-known pipe for the tobacco shop needs no further explanation. The wooden shoes, the seashells outside the shop or on the window identify and communicate a message about the service or product. If all are well designed and thoughtfully planned, the message does more: it interests and entices those who pass. The simplicity and directness of older signs often have given inspiration to contemporary designers, many of whom have used symbols and forms in ways that are excellent and timeless. Worth thinking about is the saying attributed to Samuel Taylor Coleridge, "An idea, in the highest sense of the word, cannot be conveyed but by a symbol."

1. Paul Zumther, *Daily Life in Rembrandt's Holland,* trans. from the French by Simon Watson Taylor (New York: Macmillan, 1963), pp. 6, 7.

The dolphin and anchor, a printer's mark of Aldus Manutius Romanus of Venice, 1503, was also used on inn signs found near seaports and is used today in various interpretations by printers and publishers.

The symbolic fleur-de-lys of France is often seen as a decorative element that suggests quality or excellence.

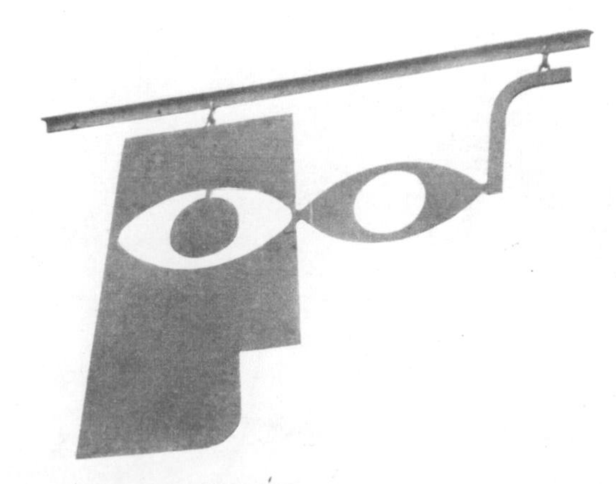

A symbol for the oculist, eyeglasses or spectacles are seen in many traditional versions and here in a contemporary interpretation hanging outside a shop in France.

FISHERMAN'S
WHARF

Inn sign—Switzerland.

Store for men—San Francisco.

Inn sign—Germany.

Vocations of the people—Munich.

Painted decorative sign—Zurich.

Swedish restaurant sign—Chicago.

Sign for antique shop—London.

Grave marker—Switzerland.

Grave marker—Switzerland.

(Page 17) Golden letters, hanging seashells, and a decorative fish make the entire window for a seafood restaurant in London an appealingly original sign.

Crest in ironwork—Bavaria.

Stone carving over entrance—Zurich.

Barber sign—Copenhagen.

Inn sign—Salzburg.

Door pulls, Italian Line—New York.

Cutlery shop—Munich.

MALMBERGS
HANDSKAR
MALMBE

This golden angel graces a large panel on the front of an apothecary shop in Switzerland.

(Left) The exquisitely sculpted form of a golden glove stands out with clarity and elegance in contrast to darker elements surrounding it on a street in Scandinavia.

A decorative sign high on a wall of an inn in Bressanone, Italy. Ornamental signs often beautify the street scene in Europe.

Inn sign—Switzerland.

Signs and pennants—Expo, Montreal.

Illuminated sign—Rotterdam.

Gourmet shop—Philadelphia.

Exhibition entrance—New York.

Restaurant sign—Boston.

Auto mechanic's shop—England.

Shoe shop—Delft, Holland.

Painted inn sign—England.

(Page 24) Construction sites often mar the cityscape; this temporary, decorative sign screened such an activity in Zurich, Switzerland.

Die Bauarbeiten dauern
bis in den Herbst 1970.
Die Eisenkonstruktion über
dem Schanzengraben
ist ein Provisorium und
wird wieder demontiert
Sie dient ausschliesslich
dem Transport des Bau-
materials.
BELAIR

2 THE FORM

Sections of musical instruments, thoughtfully arranged, inform the passerby of the nature and quality of objects to be found within. Similar setups are often found in Swiss cities.

THINGS — ACTUAL OBJECTS

The display of actual objects to inform the passerby of wares available for purchase is one of the oldest sign techniques and, no doubt, precedes actual signs. It is an important part of selling and has been since trade and barter began. Without words or with very few words, the beholder translates the object into a message that has an instant and direct appeal. Perhaps the tangible appeal is part of the attraction: it is hard to resist the colorful and pungent displays of fruits and vegetables, fragrant bouquets of flowers, or fascinating shapes and textures of antiques. Wares displayed outside a shop give direct information regarding the products within. The musical-instrument parts are evidence of the craftsmanship of the instruments for sale, while the sail tells that the boatyard is specifically for small craft.

Speaking an international language, the arrangement, shapes, sizes, and textures of vegetables in a Chinatown window in New York City act essentially as a sign.

The linear black-and-white silhouettes of objects in iron are used as symbols of the treasures to be found in this shop in France.

A hodgepodge of antique objects create an almost irresistible appeal to the collector outside a shop in New England.

OPEN
SALE

BOA YARD

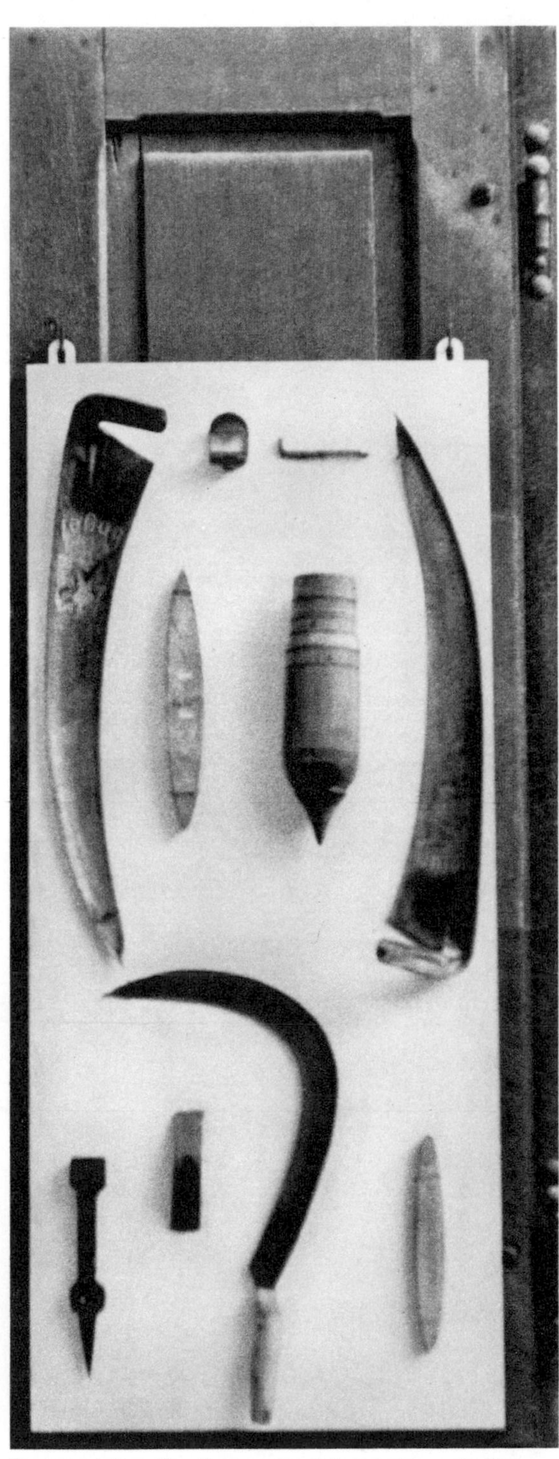

Far more interesting than a mere lettered sign, a shutter is hung with a plaque that bears an orderly display of tools of the harvest on a shop in Bressanone, Italy.

This charming arrangement of contrasting shapes and textures serves as an appealing symbol for a boutique in San Francisco.

Nautical items, including a sail blowing in the breeze, make appropriate signs for a boatyard in Boothbay Harbor, Maine.

TÜRLER

TÜRLER
TÜRLER
DAS GRÖSSTE UHREN SPEZIALGESCHÄFT DER SCHWEIZ
LE PLUS IMPORTANT MAGASIN D'HORLOGERIE DE SUISSE
SWITZERLAND'S LARGEST WATCH RETAIL SPECIALISTS

Such a handsome instrument as this one on the exterior of a shop in Zurich implies the importance and stability of "Switzerland's Largest Watch Retail Specialists."

Signs in iron have been part of the history of crafts of many countries; a decorative scroll bracket supports three crowns in hammered iron on this Italian sign of the seventeenth century. Courtesy of the Victoria and Albert Museum, London.

SYMBOLS

There is a natural sequence in the evolution of signs. First, the form is reproduced; then the form becomes a symbol of items or services offered. The symbol often is enlarged and constructed of a different material from the actual object. In the examples illustrated, the signs have been well designed with an appreciation of the original form. Enlargement as well as effective placement can aid in identification of a symbol. The beautiful bunch of grapes, the crown, the pretzel, the boot, and the key are strategically placed above doors for easy visibility from the end of the street. The giant hand for the glove shop is immediately identifiable even from a distance because of its size and the whiteness of the material. The end of the huge wine barrel speaks forcefully, hardly needing words, while the pipe door pull speaks by its very tactile use. The telephone dial and the large wooden book are simple but direct interpretations of forms, which answer the need for identification of the services offered. The use of three-dimensional construction emphasizes the image and creates a strong appeal, providing an invitation to enter and be served. Whether the symbols are from an earlier era or contemporary times, they have been carefully designed and executed for communicating an idea by the universal language of vision.

A superb example of the symbol that is often found for an establishment purveying wines in England and on the Continent.

A *coutellerie* displays this simple but elegant sign in a busy street in Sens, France.

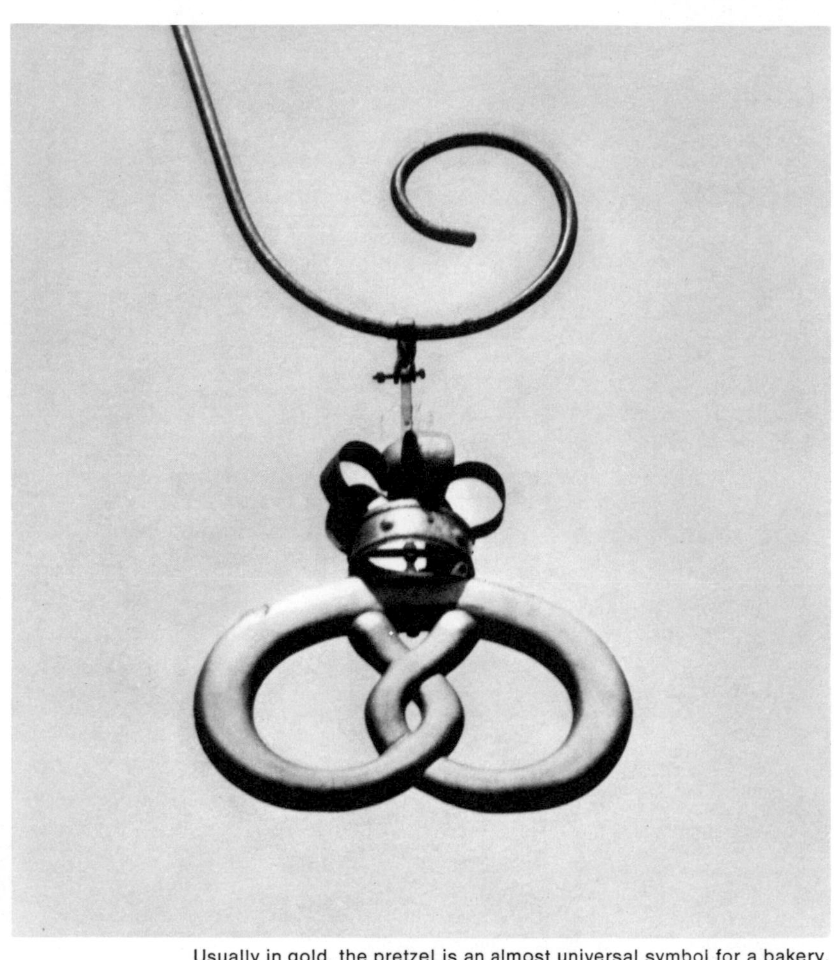

Usually in gold, the pretzel is an almost universal symbol for a bakery. This crown and pretzel identify a bakery in Copenhagen.

This handsome sign points out a store selling drapery materials and yard goods in Amsterdam.

The form of a glove, fabricated of tin and painted in bright colors, is often seen in front of shops in Europe.

Made of metal and often painted a rich red-brown, this is a symbol for tobacconists in France.

The uses of signs and symbols can often be surprising and entertaining. This beautifully crafted form is a door pull for a distinguished tobacco shop in New York City.

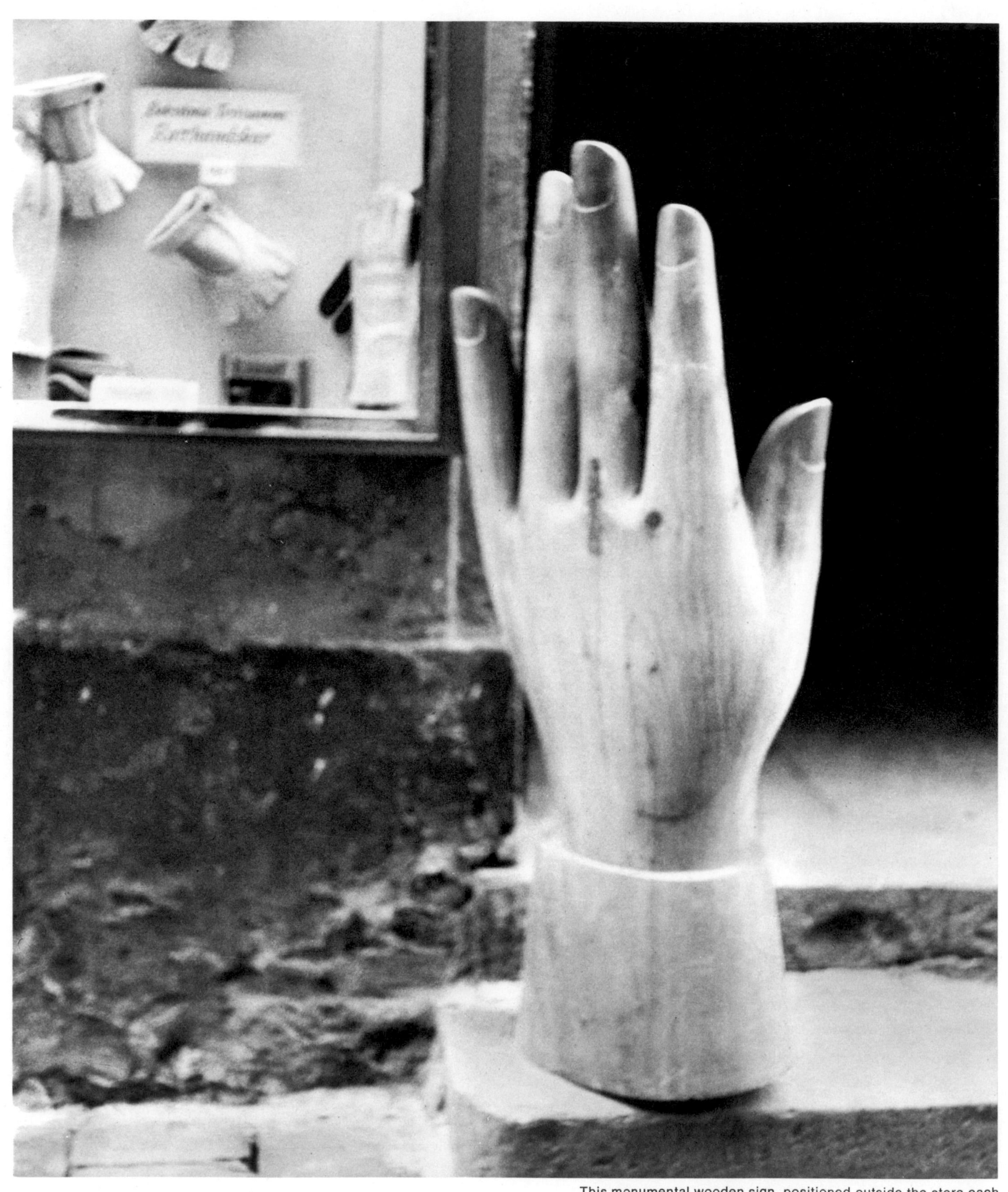

This monumental wooden sign, positioned outside the store each day, is used for drawing attention to a glove shop in Stockholm.

The craftsmanship of this golden boot speaks well for the products available in a shop in Auxerre, France.

a la botte
ZENITH

The ubiquitous teapot not only denotes a shop but is a national tradition in England and is often a welcome sign indeed.

The great, golden key has been the symbol for a locksmith for a long time. This one is on a locksmith's shop in France.

The fish has been used symbolically in both religious and secular contexts. This great, shiny fish is attached to the wall on a shop in Lancaster, England.

Revolving in the breezes of a woodland setting, this tin weathervane draws attention to a seafood restaurant on a highway in Oregon.

A bristly pig informs the passerby that all kinds of brushes made of pig's bristles are sold in this shop in England.

Though children must feel deprived by not being able to ride it, this sign has great appeal for customers of the shop in Lancaster, England.

The golden head of an animal often symbolizes the kind of meat sold in a specific shop in France. Here, pork products are indicated by the sign over a doorway in Sens.

Products of wool are symbolized by a white sheep in many English shops; this one is in Salisbury.

This sign on the front of a shop at Smithville, New Jersey, amuses and informs. It may have been inspired by one illustrated in *The Index of American Design*.

The dial and the telephone itself are effective as signs; this one is in Menaggio, Italy.

The grasshopper is the symbol of Martin's Bank, oldest bank in England, founded by Sir Thomas Gresham in 1563. This was photographed in London, and a similar sign is probably found in front of each branch of the bank.

15·TG·63

Contemporary objects, enlarged, may often be placed as symbols or signs; this big sandal of wood and leather hangs over a door in Zurich.

The simple form of a book has been used as a sign in front of a bookbinder's shop in Philadelphia.

The head of this barrel has been set into the wall of the entrance to a shop in Cheltenham, England.

Contemporary styling of office stamps is well related to the lettering on this shop in Basel, Switzerland.

Stempel

DILIGENCIA
1 REAL
POSTES
VINGT CENTS
1/10 THALER
FRANCO
DREI SGR
HANNOVER
POSTAGE
ONE PENNY
CAPE OF GOOD HOPE
STATI PARMENSI
CENTESIMI 5
STADT POST BASEL
EXPERTISE
ACHAT
ESTIMATION

An unusually handsome sign in front of a post office
in Stockholm is in excellent contrast with the architecture.

Because postage stamps are often aesthetically satisfying,
they make handsome signs on the front of this shop in Paris.

PRONTO

A small sign reduces the products to the simplest kind of symbolism and yet is most effective for a tobacco shop in Zurich.

A cup symbolizes the product and the lettering, quick service, on this sign for a chain of coffee houses in London.

A bit of decorative whimsy in wood graces the entrance to a shop for women's wear in New York City.

The sweeping forms of gulls in flight have been handsomely symbolized in this attractive sign for a restaurant in Zurich.

MÖVEN PICK

The history of signs goes back to heraldry: heraldic symbolism is often used on banners and flags. These ancient flags hang in Westminster Abbey, England.

FLAGS AND PENNANTS

Flags and pennants, in themselves signs, derive historically from heraldry and have long been used as symbols of identification and communication. Anthony Wagner and John P. Brooke-Little, English authorities on heraldry, explain its history:

> Heraldry springs from devices, boldly painted in bright colors, which knights of the first half of the twelfth century began to bear on their shields to identify them in tournament and battle. Passing from father to son the ensigns came to be thought of more as a family than purely personal possession and so became a matter of family pride and social importance . . . When Henry I of England knighted his newly wed son-in-law, Geoffrey, (called Plantagenet) Count of Anjou, in 1127, he hung about his neck a shield painted with golden lions[2]. . . These devices were painted not only on their shield but also on their horse trappings and on the loose coat worn over their armour. From this latter custom came the expression coat of arms or, more simply, just arms.[3]

Many of the old heraldic symbols have been used since those times, although there have been changes in form or design as well as interpretation. The lions or three leopards were used by the King of Gwynedd, who ruled in the counties of Anglesey, Flint, Caernarvon, and Merioneth in Wales in the early twelfth century. Today these are still to be seen in the great seal of England, the arms of the present Prince of Wales, and other arms that have been handed down from the past. The fleur-de-lys has long been associated not only with the former flag of France but with many arms of the royal and noble families of Wales as well as arms and devices seen in Florence, Italy. The fleur-de-lys is currently used by the Italian Lines. The white ostrich plumes encircled by a coronet of crosses and fleur-de-lys of the Prince of Wales is seen over doorways of shops and buildings in England. It signifies royal patronage, thus implying high quality of merchandise or service.

Flags and pennants, with their wide variety of colors and symbols, present an exciting and stirring sight when used in processions, parades, celebrations, expositions, or at public places such as the United Nations or Rockefeller Center in New York City.

The position of a flag or banner, most often overhead on a standard or pole, makes it easily seen and therefore easily recognized. In parades or celebrations, flags identify units or groups they precede. Flags or banners with various devices are used for identification at airports, on public and industrial buildings, and at special celebrations such as expositions and sports events. In many of these instances the symbol on the flag needs either very few words or none to be interpreted. Flags, banners, and pennants create special interest as signs because their waving rhythms essentially make a "sign in motion." They are especially effective when flood-lighted at night.

2. Anthony Wagner, *Heraldry in England* (Middlesex: Penguin Books, 1949), pp. 5, 6.
3. Anthony Wagner, John Brooke-Little, Rodney Dennys, and Francis Jones, *Royal and Princely Heraldry in Wales* (London: Tabard Publications, 1969), p. 7.

THE WILTSHIRE REGIMENT

In Switzerland any excuse is a good excuse for flying flags, banners, and pennants. The flags of the various cantons are often in use, as well as ones for special occasions.

Flying over a Swiss garden supply center, this flag demonstrates that simple objects can be most effectively designed for use as symbols; in this case the symbol is, appropriately, a sprouting seed.

A richly ornamented banner of many colors, which was used for a sign for an exhibition at the Hallmark Gallery in New York City, 1970.

Pennants in the form of decorative, colorful fish, flying in front of a store in the Chinese section of San Francisco, bring a festive atmosphere to the street.

SASTRERIA
DE
ALMACEN "EL CAIRO"
TROPIGAS
AGENCIA
NACIONAL
DE COBRANZAS
SUCURSAL
INFORMACION DE CREDITO
BIENES RAICES S A
TEL.-14-01
SHUKRY S. KAWAS
COMPAÑIA DE SEGUROS DE VIDA
ROBLES

Attached to the side of a white building in England, this excellent sign is enhanced by the jolly cherubs attached to it.

HUMAN FORMS

Another form with many useful aspects and possibilities of interpretation is the human figure. With almost unlimited opportunities of suggested action and position, the human form can be used to express an idea, an emotion, or a meaningful activity. There are specific instances where a human figure used without words or identification is a self-evident sign for a particular business or trade. The nautical figure still exists for this purpose; the cigar-store Indian has long since taken a place in private or museum collections. In Amsterdam, Holland, one soon becomes aware of the *gapers* (pronounced like "haypurse"), gaudily painted heads usually with their tongues sticking out, hanging above druggist shop entrances. These interesting forms were first used in Amsterdam in the seventeenth century to guide illiterate customers to the proper shop, and later appeared in Flanders.

The huge scale of these mock trousers and shirt manages to negate the clutter of other signs. Defined by electric light bulbs at night, the sign was hung over a street in San Pedro Sula, Honduras.

The fortunate position of this handsome sign, protected under a window, probably accounts, in part, for its good condition. It hangs over the doorway of one of England's oldest inns, the Angel and Royal in Grantham.

A splendid sign still in use is one of the famous *gapers* that have been the symbols of druggists' shops in Amsterdam since the seventeenth century.

For a special event, a large department store displayed enlargements, in negative form, of old prints of criers with their wares as attractive murals; Zurich, 1969.

Es ist immer etwas los bei JELMOLI
JELMOLI

Cigar-store Indians often stood before American tobacco shops but now exist mostly in museums or private collections. Carved in wood and painted in rich colors, they share the fame of the elaborately carved and decorated figureheads of sailing vessels of the same period. Courtesy of the Atwater Kent Museum in Philadelphia.

Nautical figures carved in wood have been part of the American scene for a long time. This one has been standing in front of a store selling nautical instruments and charts in Philadelphia since 1871.

RIGGS & BROTHER
Chronometers and Nautical Instruments, Agents for U.S. Government Charts

THE CROSS

The cross, or crossed lines of various kinds, has been related to religious beliefs for centuries. We still hear phrases such as "keep your fingers crossed" or "cross my heart," which evolved from a time when superstitious precautions were taken against evil spirits. When used as a symbol, the cross is more apt to signify humanitarian or religious groups. One well-known use of the cross is as the emblem of the International Red Cross organization; a white cross on a red field is Switzerland's flag; a white cross with lines extending to the borders of the red flag becomes the flag of Denmark. For religious use the cross is interpreted on churches, chapels, vestments, banners, chalices, and other religious objects, as well as on hallowed ground and in cemeteries.

Grave markers in the form of wood or metal crosses, some quite humble in their craftsmanship, others more elaborate, are still to be found in *camposantos* (cemeteries) in New Mexico.

In Switzerland the cross is used in almost every kind of material and form, often showing elaborate craftsmanship, as in this one in Latterbrunnen.

Elisabeth

This simple, dignified cross is in perfect harmony with the contemporary architecture of the church near which it stands in New England.

Signs on architecture must be well related to the structure, as is this cross on the Cathedral at Coventry, England.

3 UNCLASSIFIED FORMS

The examples of signs grouped under the heading "Unclassified Forms" are not of a single tradition or form but of a composite group of skills and creative ideas. Each is unique and almost defies classification. In some, the designer, whether trained or untrained, had an original and sensitive perception for making use of texture and material that would be relevant to his message. In others, a logical use of the available surface, such as the side of a building or a lunette over a doorway, offered opportunity for the needed symbol or letters. A play upon words to express the names of owners of property gave the signmaker a chance to use symbols to represent the syllables of words, as in rebus writing in children's books and blocks.

In some of these examples there is evidence of sophistication, judgment, and a real knowledge of design, whether the letters are created by growing plants or obtained by an unusual technique employed to hold loosely draped fabric over simple and powerful letters during construction work on a building. On the other hand, the direct but unsophisticated use of pebbles to create a sign for a seaside restaurant and the use of the back of a building for a map of a nearby ski run are intelligent and effective ways to employ the material at hand.

No single rule seems applicable to all the effective ways that signs communicate their messages. An analysis of what makes a good sign involves many different judgments. In a report published by The Eastern Arts Association it was said that, "A sign may simply inform or direct, but it may also be designed to demand an active aesthetic response."[4] The viewer, all too often, is unconscious of this aesthetic aspect of signs and symbols. He may also be unaware of the efficiency and quality of them as designs. A sensitive eye for good letter forms, for composition and organization of forms within an area, for the forms' relationship to the background, and for the building or space will help the viewer appreciate a sign's aesthetic potential.

Following no set tradition and using no obvious ways and means, each of the examples in this chapter was created by a designer whose fresh and vital approach solved the problem in an ingenuous and memorable manner. Some of the signs are old, some new; some use folk-art techniques while some have been designed for more sophisticated needs and standards. They are reminders that, in any age, the sincere and able designer or craftsman uses the media of his time that are at hand, in an honest and direct effort to communicate his ideas.

4. The Eastern Arts Association, "Art Education for Scientist and Engineer" (Report of the Committee for the Study of the Visual Arts at the Massachusetts Institute of Technology, 1957.)

The sign of the Three Crowns Tavern, dating back to 1771, is still in existence as a piece of decor in the lobby of the Sheraton-Conestoga Motor Inn near Lancaster, Pennsylvania. The seven bullet holes visible in the sign attest to the marksmanship of American soldiers who suspected the keeper of the tavern of Tory sentiments.

Designers are often puzzled by the problem of fitting a given number of letters on a given line length; the painter of this quaint wooden sign, which hangs in the Pennsylvania Farm Museum, Lancaster, Pennsylvania, was caught in the same dilemma.

A very simple organization of elements produced this decorative iron sign for an American, nineteenth-century butcher shop. Courtesy of the Atwater Kent Museum, Philadelphia.

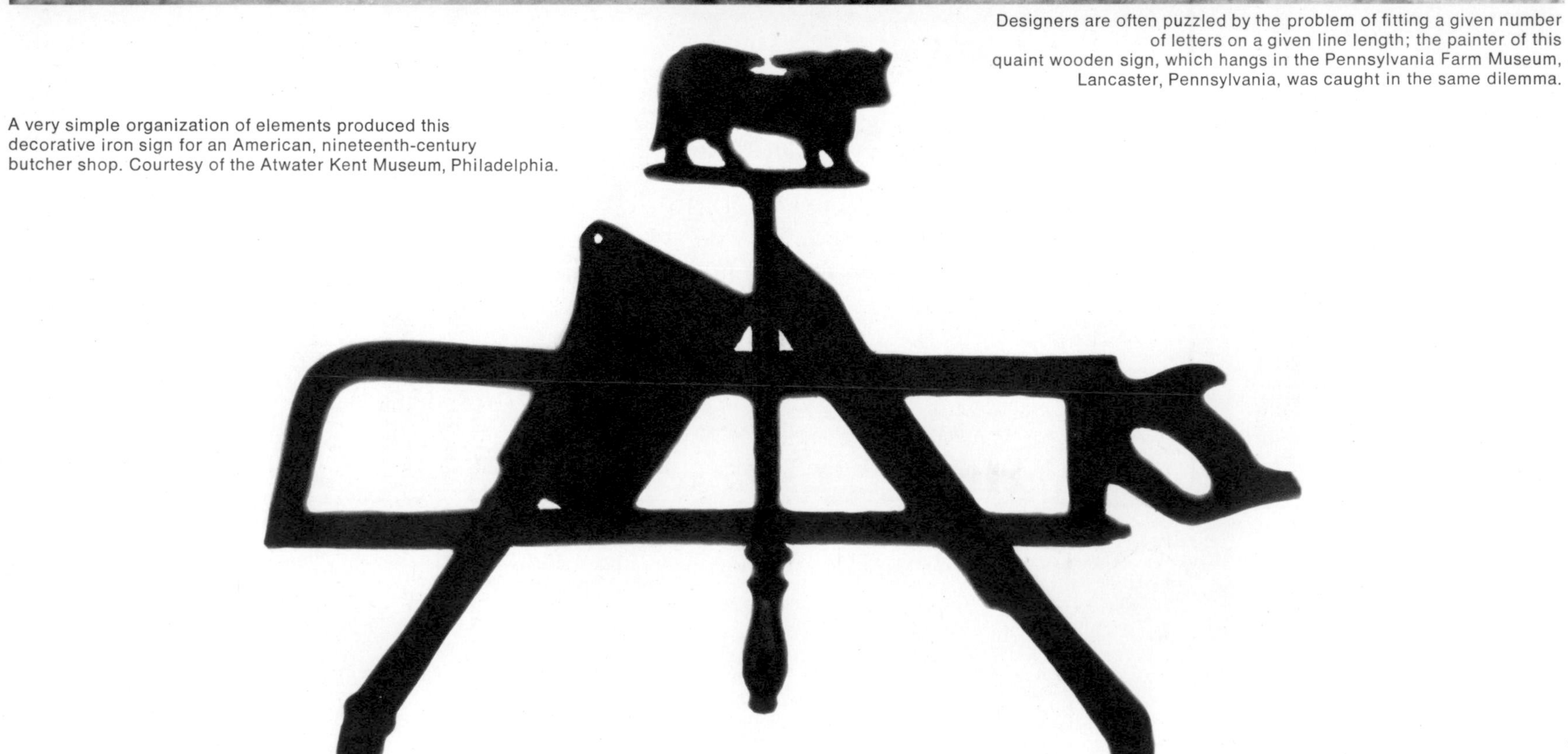

This simple, forthright sign made of wood is protected from the weather in an admirably simple way. The sign is attached to a building formerly used as a courthouse in New England.

FORMER
U.S. COURT HOUSE.
HERE ON NOV. 7, 1860
JUDGE A.G. MAGRATH
LEFT THE BENCH
DIVESTED HIMSELF
OF HIS JUDICIAL
ROBES AND DECLARED
THAT THE TEMPLE
OF JUSTICE IS
NOW CLOSED.

It is apparent that the owner of this farm has lively interests besides agriculture; it is fortunate that his name and some of his equipment suited his purposes.

The back of a very ordinary building becomes interesting by a sign — actually a map — for ski runs on the Mohawk Trail in Massachusetts.

R STEIGER
FASSHANDEL

Signs and symbols of a temporary nature can be as compelling and entertaining as more permanent ones. This temporary sign was placed in front of the Museum of Contemporary Crafts in New York City.

A dealer in metal drums saw an opportunity for the use of existing shapes and took full and intriguing advantage of it, incidentally decorating this highway in Switzerland.

Hanging under the porch roof of a shop in Albuquerque, New Mexico, this sign has a very personalized feeling, and works well with the architecture.

Straw, a common packaging material, is appropriately used in a sign for a wine-dispensing establishment in Bavaria.

This sign made of bits of driftwood is a real surprise at a men's restroom along the rugged coast of northern California.

A visual pun on the owner's name makes a sign for a house in the Pocono Mountains of Pennsylvania. Fortunately, the name fitted the contours of an attractive bird silhouette.

Made of stones pressed into concrete, this is an appropriate sign for a seafood restaurant on the coast of northern California.

asgrow

This huge draped sign was an ingenious soiution to a common problem: how to give information while taking away the curse of construction during the renovation of a building in New York City.

Though overly elaborate signs made of plants and flowers are sometimes seen in town centers, here growing things delineate the trademark of an agricultural products manufacturer in a sign that is harmonious to the surroundings.

Sandpiper Village

Derived from the decorative ironwork signs of the past, this antique auto wheel is properly suited to an antique automobile shop.

Although signs for real estate developments are seldom good, this one carved in a redwood log is appropriate to its West Coast location.

4 THE DECORATIVE SIGN

In addition to guiding, informing, warning, and amusing us, signs and symbols also decorate and enliven our surroundings. In certain places signs are prohibited by ordinance, because they do not fulfill their decorative functions or because too many competing signs produce visual confusion and, sometimes, safety hazards. When huge outdoor advertising signs spoil the vistas of nature, they should be restricted: the scenic view from the highway should not be obliterated by man-made signs. However, decoratively suitable signs on city streets and village byways add to the scene handsome and delightful notes that seem to be missing in many newly built areas. In some cities and towns, the decorative sign has taken on a classic quality that is timeless in its elegance.

In the narrow streets of old European cities one may see many familiar symbols of the past used with great variety and charm: kings and crowns to remind the traveler of royal meetings, royal or noble patronage, or even of the three Magi; the key, symbol of St. Peter, to stand for hospitality or for, perhaps, a locksmith; the star, the anchor, the rose, the bunch of grapes or wine glass, or the eagle of St. John (later the symbol of the Holy Roman Empire) to call familiar associations or memories to mind. Pilgrims and other travelers, often on hazardous journeys, were reassured when they saw inn signs bearing symbols that had meaning for them. The sign might be a combination of historic and religious symbols or the older meanings might have been lost in time and replaced with new interpretations. In decorative signs, however, the whole sign is more important than the symbol itself. It is apt to be interesting, unusual, and eye-catching. Supporting brackets of great beauty and delicacy, well balanced to accent and harmonize with symbols, often show evidence of a high degree of skill. Many were designed by jewelers and by metalsmiths working in silver and in wrought iron. The embellishments or details of the brackets or other supports may include, in addition to rhythmic curves, such forms as the head of an eagle or hawk, a graceful design of wreaths, swags of metal drapery, leaves, flowers, acorns and other objects artfully incorporated to provide a rich setting that enhances the whole sign. Each example is completely individual: there are no two alike, and each seems evidence of enthusiasm, skill, and artistry accomplished by the creative use of metal.

One must realize that the ornately decorative sign is beautiful and elegant only when suitably related to its purpose and surroundings; when attempted by less able artisans who copy the old styles with little knowledge, spirit, appreciation, or sensitivity, the result can be tawdry and cheap. In a preface to a book on signs, Werner Kaempfen has written, "there must be no sham sentiment about nature, no romanticism propped up by technical science; neither must we replace the old, simple inn signs by copies in an artificial traditional style."[5] The real charm of these signs, which combine meaningful symbols and decoration, results from individual inventiveness, ingenuity, knowledge of basic tradition, decorative imagination, and the complete sincerity of the signmaker.

5. René Creux, *Old Inn Signs in Switzerland* (Lausanne: Paudex, 1962), p. 8.

A wrought-iron brewer's sign, made in South Germany in the eighteenth-century, is described as, "A wreath of hops enclosing a spray of barley with maltster's ladle and shovel crossed in saltire; bunches of ribands above and below; to the lower part of the wreath is hung a label." Courtesy of the Victoria and Albert Museum, London.

Beautifully crafted signs such as this one still grace
the streets and byways of Switzerland and neighboring countries.

The medallion on an unusually ornate metal sign hanging in front of an antique shop in
Chester, England, does not carry the name of the shop, but the date *1889*
can be seen as a part of the elegant design.

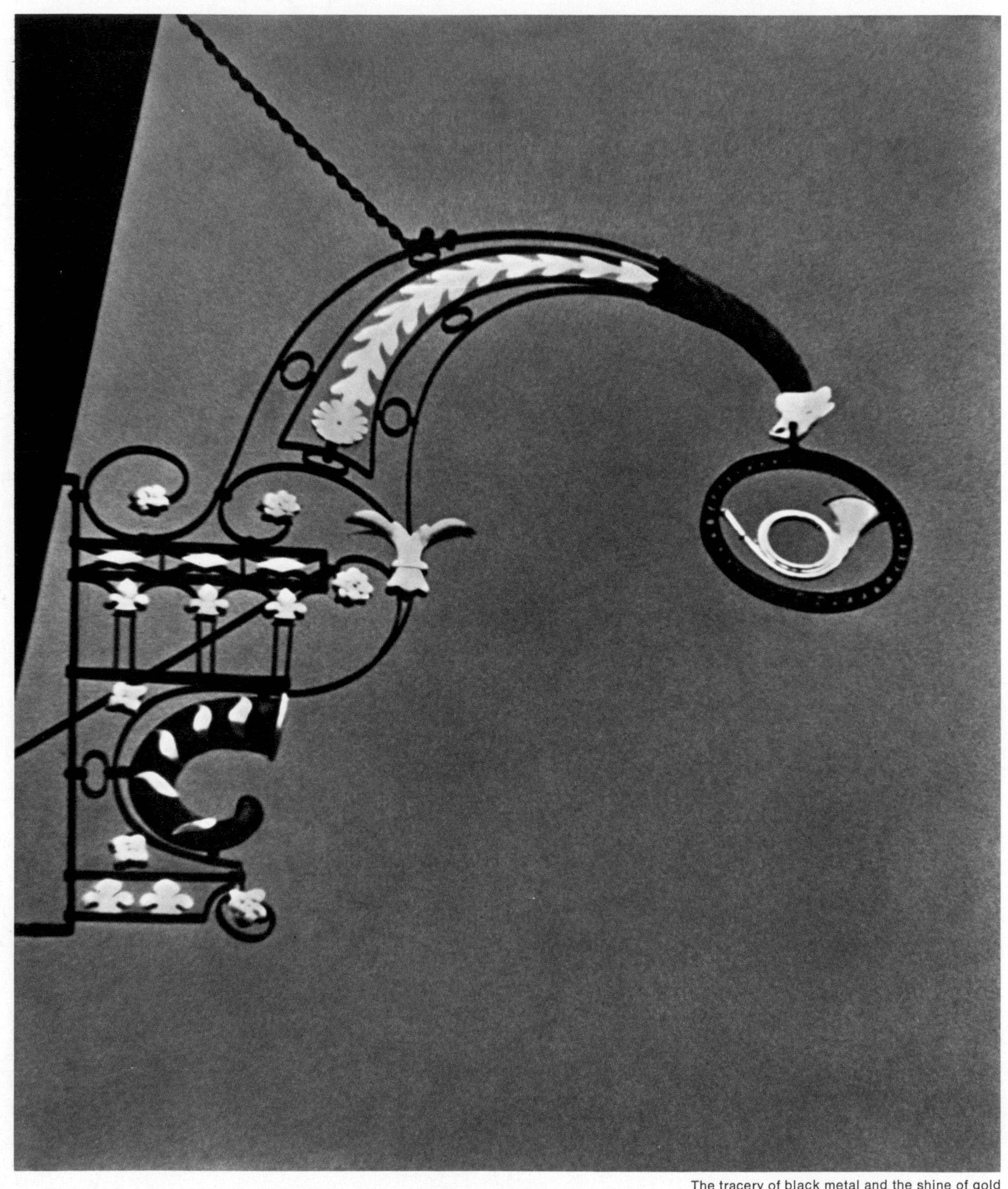

The tracery of black metal and the shine of gold are typical of many signs in Switzerland.

Because the ornate support of this sign seems heavier than is required, one surmises that it may have been used for a larger sign at an earlier time.

The head of an eagle is often an important feature of the decorative supports in signs seen in Austria, Switzerland, and surrounding areas. (Note that the support and the sign are even more decorative than previous examples shown.)

Historically, the crown symbolized royal patronage, but in contemporary usage it suggests quality or excellence. This golden crown contrasts with dull metal in a sign for an inn in Switzerland.

HOTEL
GOLDENER GREIF

Contemporary letters in neon, seen on the building in the lower left corner, break the charming effect of this elaborate sign that graces, surprisingly, the front of a bank in Germany.

Gold and black are intricately interspersed in this extremely decorative sign in Austria.

A basic star motif is displayed on a street renowned for many old-world signs by a brewery in Salzburg, Austria.

The decorative border on this sign is an excellent foil for the sharp, angular quality of the golden star on this sign in Switzerland.

The golden sun motif surrounded by black metalwork that enhances its brightness is an eye-pleasing combination. This sign was found in Austria.

The shape of a golden sun surrounds other objects on a sign in Innsbruck.

A profusion of decorative elements are found in the many signs on a Salzburg street famed for ornamental signs.

1889
Alois
Mainx
1929
GLASEREI

5 MATERIALS AND FABRICATION

In signs, as well as other art forms, the selection of materials bears a direct relationship to their use. Signs can be fabricated from a great variety of materials—wood, metal, glass or plastic, to name a few. They can be made attractive and vigorous by sculptural effects, paint, illumination. The methods of fabrication should relate to the intended idea, action, product, or service the sign proclaims, as well as to the situation and location in which the sign is placed.

WOOD

Because of its more or less universal availability, wood has been a natural choice in the making of signs over a long period of time and in many countries. With relatively simple tools and methods, wood can be carved, formed, incised, and painted, and its easy workability allows for the use of forms other than the square or rectangle. Grain and texture are often used to good decorative advantage, whether the surface is left in its natural state or treated with special finishes. In many wood signs on taverns, inns, shops, as well as in figureheads for ships and cigar-store Indians, the material was carved in relief or in the round; the sculptural potential of wood lent itself to the three-dimensional interpretations of sign ideas by artist and craftsman.

Constructed mostly of wood, this contemporary sign has been carefully designed to harmonize with the Colonial architecture of a street in Philadelphia.

TANCREDI
APOTHECARY

The pineapple has long been used in architecture and furniture as a symbol of hospitality.
The feeling of days gone by is captured in this wood sign in Massachusetts.

The rustic quality of this hanging sign is appropriate to a museum displaying objects of past eras in New England.

This wood sign is interestingly constructed, but the whole ensemble could have been improved by better rendering of lantern and lettering.

1
WATERVILLE ROAD
IDC
INDUSTRIAL DESIGN CONSULTANTS

This simple white sign is of wood with the exception of the facing panel, which is of plastic; lettering has been silk-screened in reverse on the back of the panel to preserve it from the elements. The sign has been detailed to relate to the Colonial architecture of the church, which dates back to 1761, in Philadelphia.

The oval form of this wood sign in Connecticut is unique, and suggests the possibility of using it as a posting board in a town square. The lettering, unfortunately, could be better.

Delightful texture, unusual lettering, and a shape with great character make this appealing sign in wood; it is one of many on a street of fine examples in San Francisco.

Another sign on the same street in San Francisco. All of the elements are satisfying, except for an unfortunately characterless method of support.

A large covered walkway built of wood (its design signifying that another hotel was being added to the Hyatt House chain) enlivened the area and protected pedestrians during a construction project in San Francisco.

JOHN Mc CANN.

A metal rose hangs from the ceiling of a shopping arcade in Innsbruck.

IRON

From the solid, direct form of the hitching post to the almost lacelike signs of Switzerland and other European countries, cast iron and wrought iron have provided opportunities to develop signs with both structural strength and a wide variety of delicate forms. The interpretation of design ideas in iron has resulted in achievements of great charm and artistic merit; the finest examples relate in all ways—form, structure, detail—to the purposes for which they were intended.

The sign of a blacksmith, often exhibiting a horseshoe or other examples of his craftsmanship, was obviously related to the product. Handsome decorative signs for old inns created a vivid impression of the hospitality and charm within; happily many old inn signs are still in use. Contemporary iron signs may show the form of a pretzel, a sunburst, or other familiar objects.

Hitching posts are useful only as decorative objects in contemporary life, but the lesson of beautiful letters neatly applied to objects still stands in this solid iron hitching post on the grounds of the Shelburne Museum in Vermont.

A blacksmith shop, no longer in use, still supports this wonderful handmade wrought-iron sign in the Pennsylvania countryside.

Evidence of fine craftsmanship in iron is shown by this elaborate sign for an ironworker and blacksmith in France.

A contemporary sign successfully catches the character of old-time ironwork in Greenfield, Massachusetts.

A horseshoe with decorative ironwork suggests various activities at the forge in this shop in Cheltenham, England.

Often carved in wood and finished in gold leaf, the pretzel is given an admirably simple interpretation in this metal bakery sign in Basel, Switzerland.

This contemporary use of the sun symbol, in flat metal with excellent script letters, relates beautifully to an ironwork gate nearby in Montreal.

La Boutique
430

GOLDBEATERS HOUSE

Handcarved in a rugged slab of wood, this sign bears incised letters that are gold leafed, or painted in gold.

SILVER, GOLD AND OTHER METALS

Silver and gold have often been used not only to give contrast to other materials such as wood and iron, but to lend a sense of elegance to the whole. Such materials are specially effective because their reflectivity enhances the effect of light itself, adding to the sign's visual appeal; they can often be seen at greater distances than other materials. Sculptured forms such as figures, animals and other objects are, even though excellent in themselves, enhanced by the applications of gold or silver leaf. The golden head on a French *boucherie* specifies which meat is available within.

Letter forms can be treated or finished in gold or silver either as flat characters or as elegantly formed, three-dimensional letters and scripts; the materials enhance the character and definition of the chosen letter forms. In many instances gold or silver letters are used in relief, so light plays on more than one facet of the form.

Appropriately shiny in bright gold, this symbol becomes a part of the decor on a building in London.

大同飯店

The flounder, not the most beautiful of fish, is contoured here
in shining gold to produce an elegant sign; Basel, Switzerland.

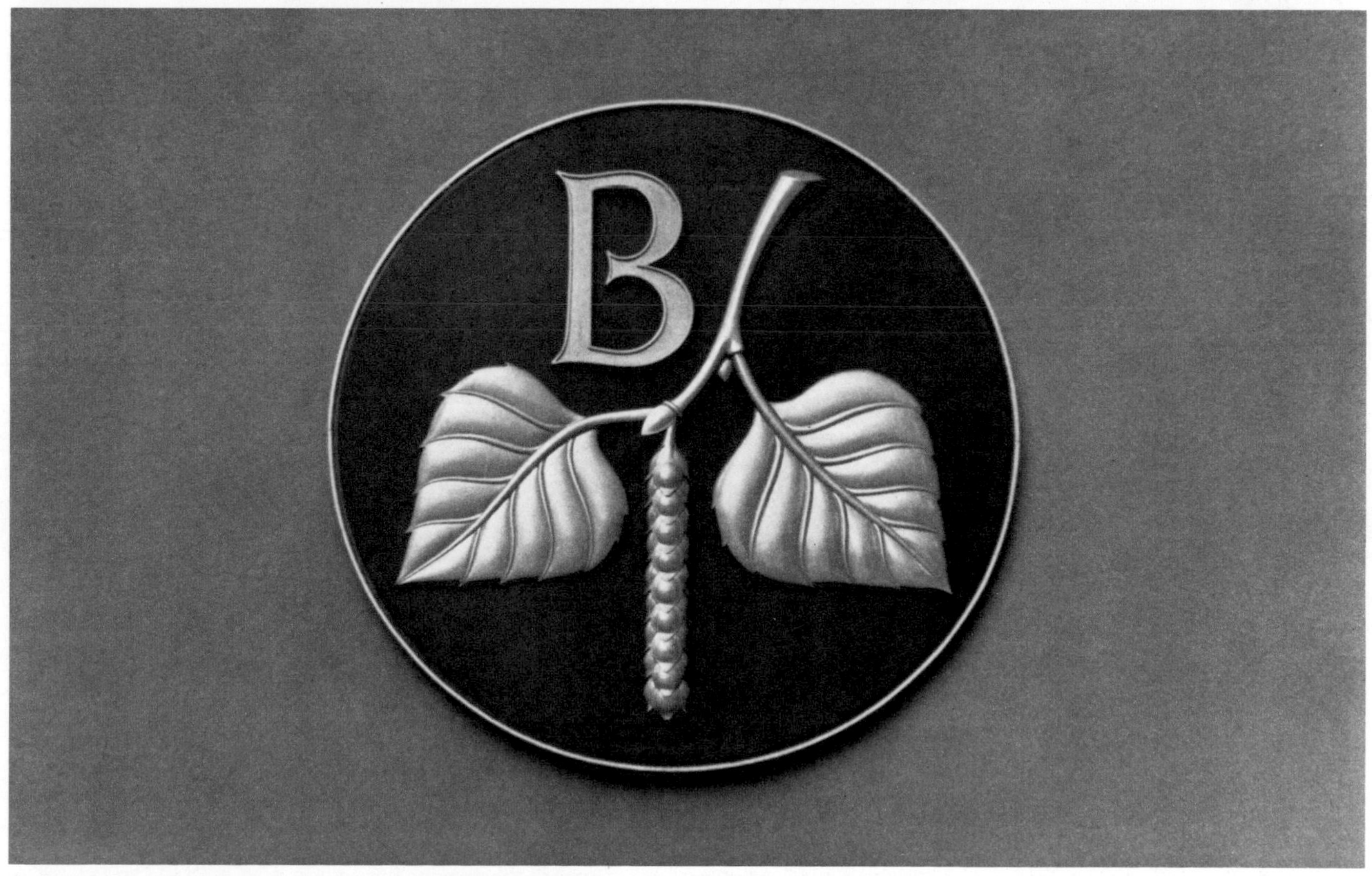

A circular sign with the same treatment as the sign above, found
in Basel, a city distinguished for an unusual number of excellent signs.

Set against a simple, dark wood background, these plaques with
Chinese characters stand out handsomely in shining gold in Seattle.

A small but most distinguished gold sign with reliefwork; Basel, Switzerland.

A classic style of Roman lettering in gold, mounted on rich red-brown, lends great distinction to this sign for an antique shop in San Francisco.

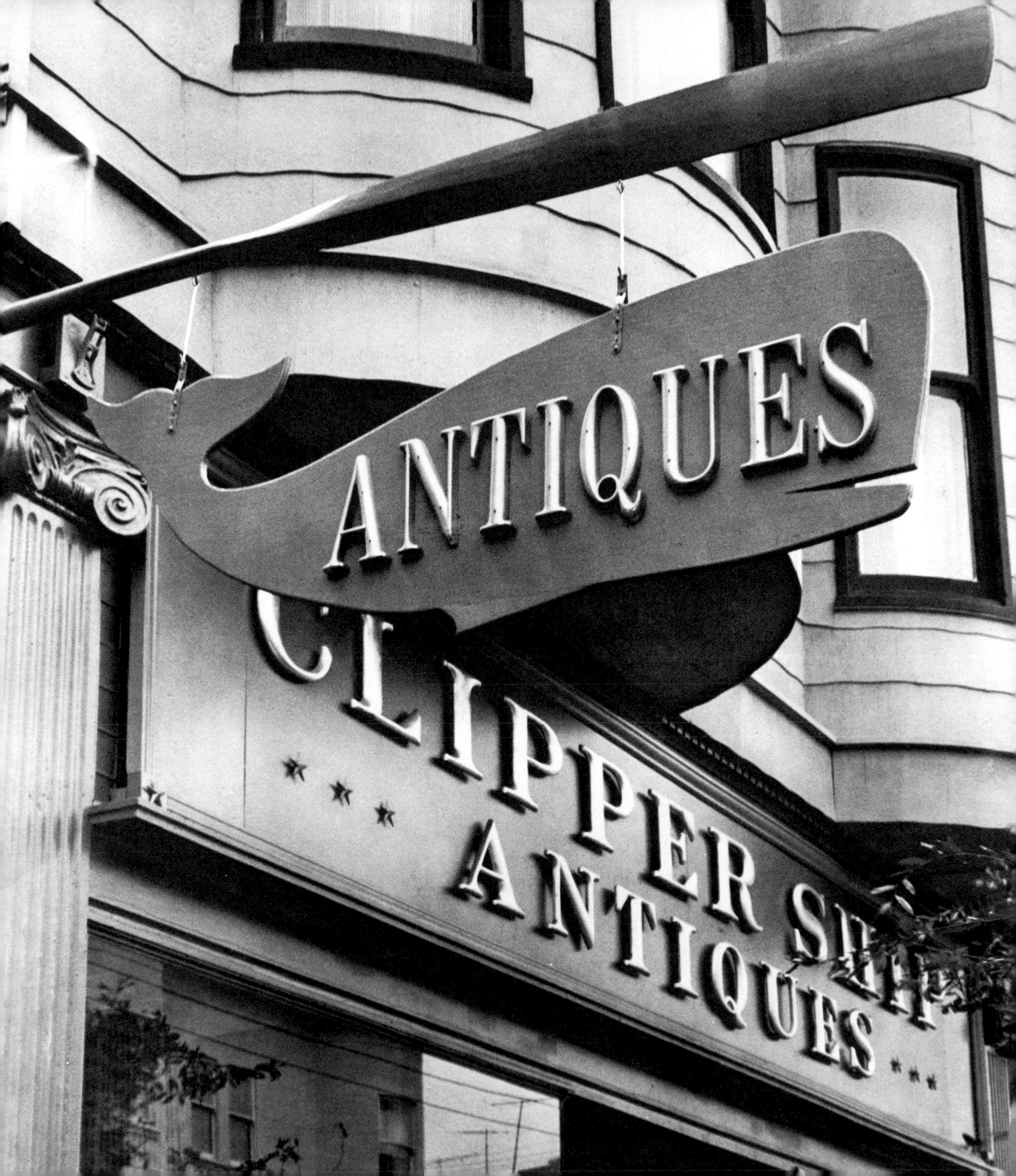
ANTIQUES
CLIPPER
ANTIQUES

Signs in gold on the front of a firehouse capture something of the feeling of old-time fire apparatus. Painted a rich New England barn red with white trim, this is in Newcastle, Maine.

Very elegant letters in gold stand out from the background panel. The sign gives an indication of the quality of merchandise to be found in this store in Seattle.

The contemporary use of symbols is apparent in this London bank's symbol; it is executed on plastic on the small sign and in aluminum or stainless steel on the contrasting black wall.

The Royal Bank
of Scotland

The painted or pictorial sign constructed of wood is still in evidence in England. The golden fighting cock is the symbol of Courage, a large English brewing company.

A charming picture is painted on this sign beside the highway between London and Cambridge, England.

PAINT AND PICTURE

One objective of a sign is to give information quickly and simply. Even as late as 1825, about one-third of the population of the United States could not read. Painted and pictorial inn signs flourished in the late seventeenth, eighteenth, and early nineteenth centuries. Thus, the painted sign, the simple direct image, spoke without words or, at least, with very few words. In some instances the painted sign was supported by, and embellished with, decorative wrought iron or even a sculptured form such as the Courage Breweries' symbol of the cock in Britain. The traditional inn signs of Switzerland, Germany, Austria, Bavaria, France, and Britain, as well as the United States, were distinctive of their particular areas, and many had great charm and simplicity. It is interesting to note that some great painters also painted signs.

In addition to separately hung or mounted signs, the outside walls of buildings have been embellished with painted letters and decorative and figurative forms proclaiming the inn, the wine cellar, the residence of a famous citizen or even the occupations of a town.

England's great traditions of the sea often appear on inn signs in such names as Ship or Anchor; this one apparently memorializes a particular ship.

This sign is hand-painted with great care and detail; it was made for one of a large chain of hotels and inns in England.

The design is probably silk-screened on the flat surface of this small sign. The ironwork is in perfect harmony with the sign itself; Zurich.

A sign with a decorative star motif stands before an inn selling the products of another large brewing company in England.

A historic custom that still exists is pictured on a sign for The Ring-O-Bells Inn in England.

Gut und echt Gilt als recht

Rast Sei willkommen uns als lieber Gast

Hotel

Der Seestern grüsst

den

Bietet

Haus

Throughout Switzerland one finds areas of architecture used
for a sign or ornament, or both; this fine example is in Zurich.

The entire front of this hotel in the countryside of Switzerland has become a huge
hand-painted, decorative sign. Certainly one senses a feeling of warm hospitality for the guests.

Exterior walls of buildings in many Central European countries are painted with figures and lettering spatially well related to the architecture. The figures often indicate the occupations of the area.

An extremely simple piece of architecture is made more interesting by a frieze of two lines of well-executed lettering.

Every detail of the lettering and the sign is thoughtfully conceived and executed at this establishment on a street corner in Zurich.

Veltliner
Veltliner
Keller

Appropriately decorative letters on the inside of the glass of a small showcase made an excellent sign for an exhibition at the Hallmark Galleries in New York City.

GLASS OR WINDOW

Today we are accustomed to glass display windows and to glass lobby doors. The window attests to the validity of the ideas expressed earlier in this book that objects on display and for sale are, in effect, signs. The display window and the door are often used as signs, supplementing signage above and around the window, and bringing pertinent information into closer visual range of the passing observer.

Painted, gold-leafed, or adhered letters or symbols have all been used successfully on glass. One remembers windows with glorious gold letters, sometimes ornate, sometimes plain, mounted on the glass and often arranged in a circular arch. What wonders the shopper expected within such a store!

Temporary or permanent signs are often displayed inside glass windows, and occasionally the window itself becomes the basis for a well-designed temporary sign or symbol, or a bit of lighthearted but pertinent whimsy.

A glass window showing artifacts and reproductions is advantageously used at the entrance to a museum in Ravenna, Italy.

MVSEO

Es bueno - es danes
Det er god

A strip of paper used as the background for well-designed and executed script lettering became the sign for an antique shop in Philadelphia.

Attractively decorated windows using a variety of lettering, artwork and foods became, in effect, one big sign presenting Danish products in Copenhagen.

Gegen
Engerlinge
Basudin®
Emulsion
giessen
Geigy

The lettering on this entrance door, without becoming cheap or gaudy, carries a wealth of information, and its design relates well to the architecture of the building in Zurich.

Nature forms and lettering made a striking graphic panel on plastic or glass, hanging inside a window of a seedsman's store in Switzerland.

Glass show windows offer an excellent opportunity for signs, particularly when they are as well achieved as these examples in London and in Zurich.

A whimsical, lighthearted use of a glass show window, which leaves no doubt of its message in Amsterdam.

LIGHT — PLASTIC AND NEON

For many years light has been used simply as a means of focusing attention on a sign. With the development of newer illuminating methods and materials, light has become a creative element in the art of signmaking. Unfortunately it is too often used in an inartistic manner, and a badly designed illuminated sign has often replaced an older, more beautiful sign. Serenity and elegance have been lost in an effort to be up-to-date. But the judicious use of light, whether the source be incandescent, neon, fluorescent, or anything more recently developed by modern technology, is beginning to bring about an increasing number of well-designed illuminated signs. These are simple and direct, easily read at a distance or in a short space of time, use well-planned letters or symbols, and are not visually irritating. In these, the combinations of light, form, and color have been utilized with careful consideration of the message, the environment in which the signs are placed, and the possibility of immediate optical and aesthetic reception.

Developed only recently, plastic materials have almost too literally burst upon the street and highway. As a whole, their contribution to urban and roadside beauty has been minimal. It needs to be said that the insensitive use of plastics and neon, together with cheap gaudiness and bad lettering, have done much to create the ill will of the public for signs in general.

This is unfortunate. Plastics have much to offer the signmaker in ease of fabrication, adaptability to illumination, relative indestructibility (they often take the place of breakable glass) and wide color range. The situation is not hopeless. Now and then one sees signs made of plastic, in combination with other materials and illumination, that pass every standard of visibility, acceptability and good taste.

Although not dated, this sign made of metal tubing may have been one of the earliest attempts at illuminating in the manner of contemporary neon lighting: it contains tiny holes which showed light, as illuminating gas flowed through the hollow tubing. It is said that the sign was used as a nocturnal welcome sign on Independence Hall in Philadelphia. Courtesy of the Atwater Kent Museum, Philadelphia.

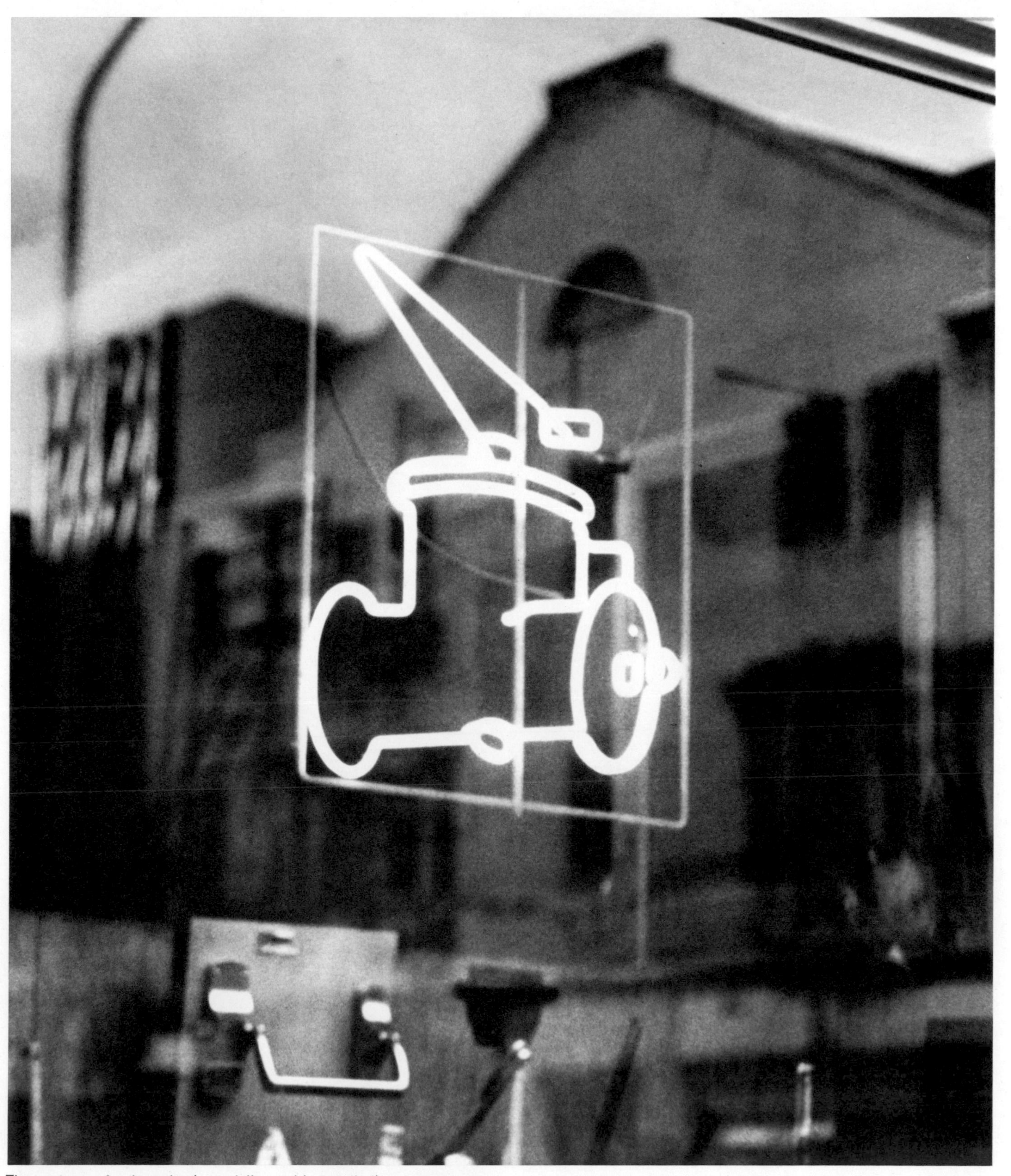

The contours of a door check are delineated in exactly the same manner as the gas-illuminated eagle except that neon tubing is used, not metal.

MÉTRO

Handsome in itself, and enhanced by beautiful backlighting, this is the symbol of a post office in Stockholm.

This excellent example of a simple illuminated sign points the way to entrances to the underground transportation system in Montreal.

YOU'RE RIGHT!
IT'S WOOLMARK
PURE WOOL

YOU'RE RIGHT!
IT'S WOOLMARK
PURE WOOL

YOU'RE RIGHT!
IT'S WOOLMARK
PURE WOOL

YOU'RE RIGHT!
IT'S WOOLMARK
PURE WOOL

Beautiful lettering makes possible the simple and tasteful neon illumination of the logo of a Milan department store.

The flashing of electrically lighted signs is not always pleasant to the eyes. The contemporary symbol for products made of wool has been intelligently developed in a sign on Broadway, New York City; the five sequential stages of the illumination of the sign are shown in the five reproductions at the left.

This little sign over a door pull, which may conceivably be one of the most beautiful "keep out" signs in the world, was found in Zurich.

6 LETTERING AND NUMERALS

A number of signs shown in this book have no lettering on them and do not require a written word. When the message can be told instantly with a symbol or simple form, the sign's function is complete. Most signs, however, require additional information, and the use of lettering is the only adequate complement to other design elements. It is also possible to have an excellent sign where the design features are letter or numeral forms alone.

Lettering itself is an art. It requires a thorough knowledge of the history and anatomy of letters, great design ability, and facility in the actual making of the letters themselves. As with so many art forms, the novice or amateur thinks that he is able to produce accomplished lettering; it is small wonder, then, that we see so many signs in which the lettering is distinctly poor. The examples in this section show that letters and numerals can have great character and visual interest. All are very legible, and in some the letters have been developed into comprehensive and intriguing designs. The lettering on signs throughout this book should prove that no matter how letters are produced, in many kinds of materials and techniques and applied to all kinds of backgrounds, the significant design factors are the taste and appropriateness with which they have been chosen.

Love for beautiful decoration is shown by the use of well-designed and well-executed lettering in Zurich.

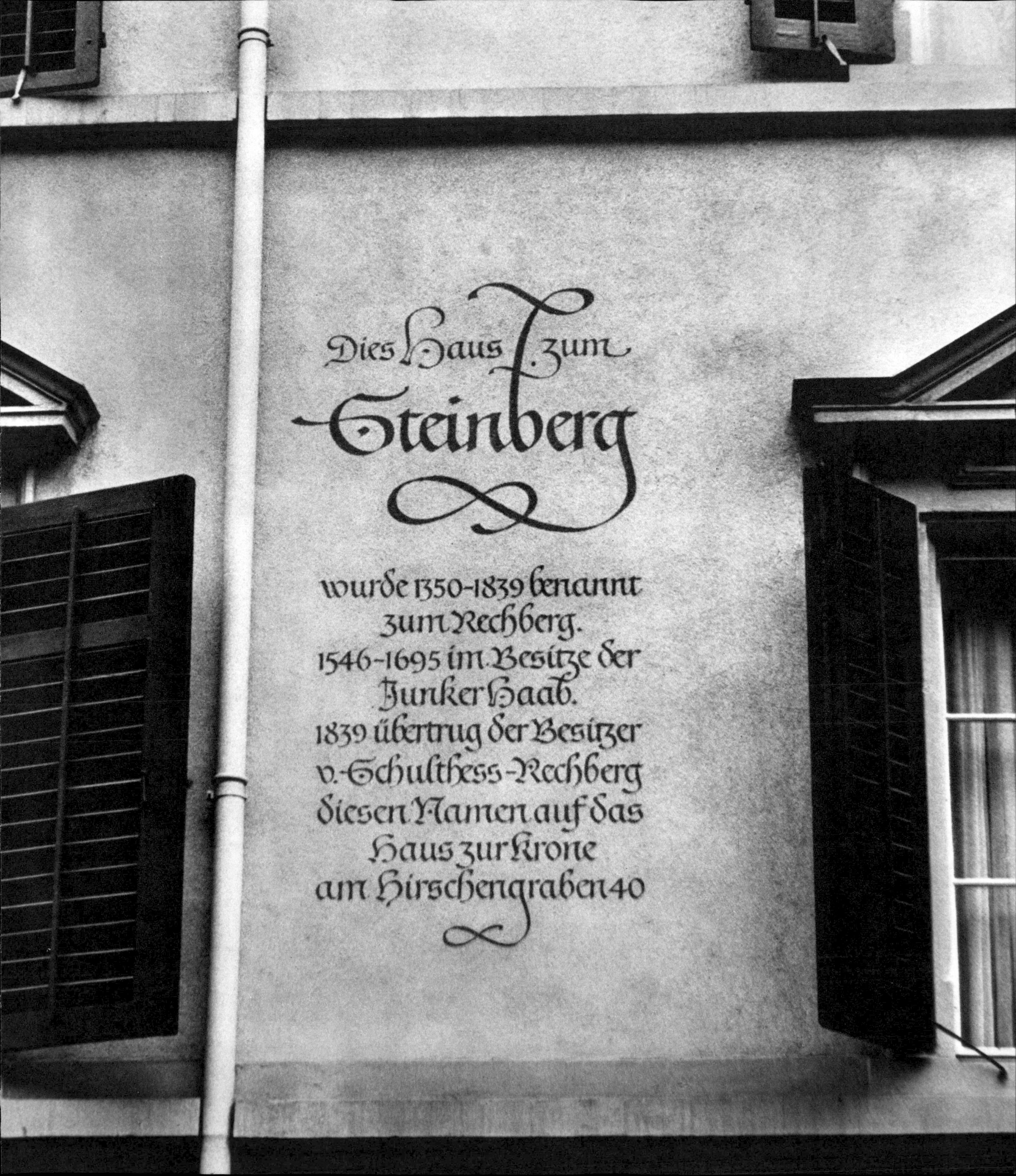
Dies Haus zum
Steinberg
wurde 1350-1839 benannt
zum Rechberg.
1546-1695 im Besitze der
Junker Haab.
1839 übertrug der Besitzer
v.-Schulthess-Rechberg
diesen Namen auf das
Haus zur Krone
am Hirschengraben 40

Simple, contemporary letters on glass, related to the architectural interior, are praiseworthy in this gallery in Stockholm.

The well-known trademark initial of Knoll furniture is shown here, strategically placed in the garden entrance to a showroom in Philadelphia.

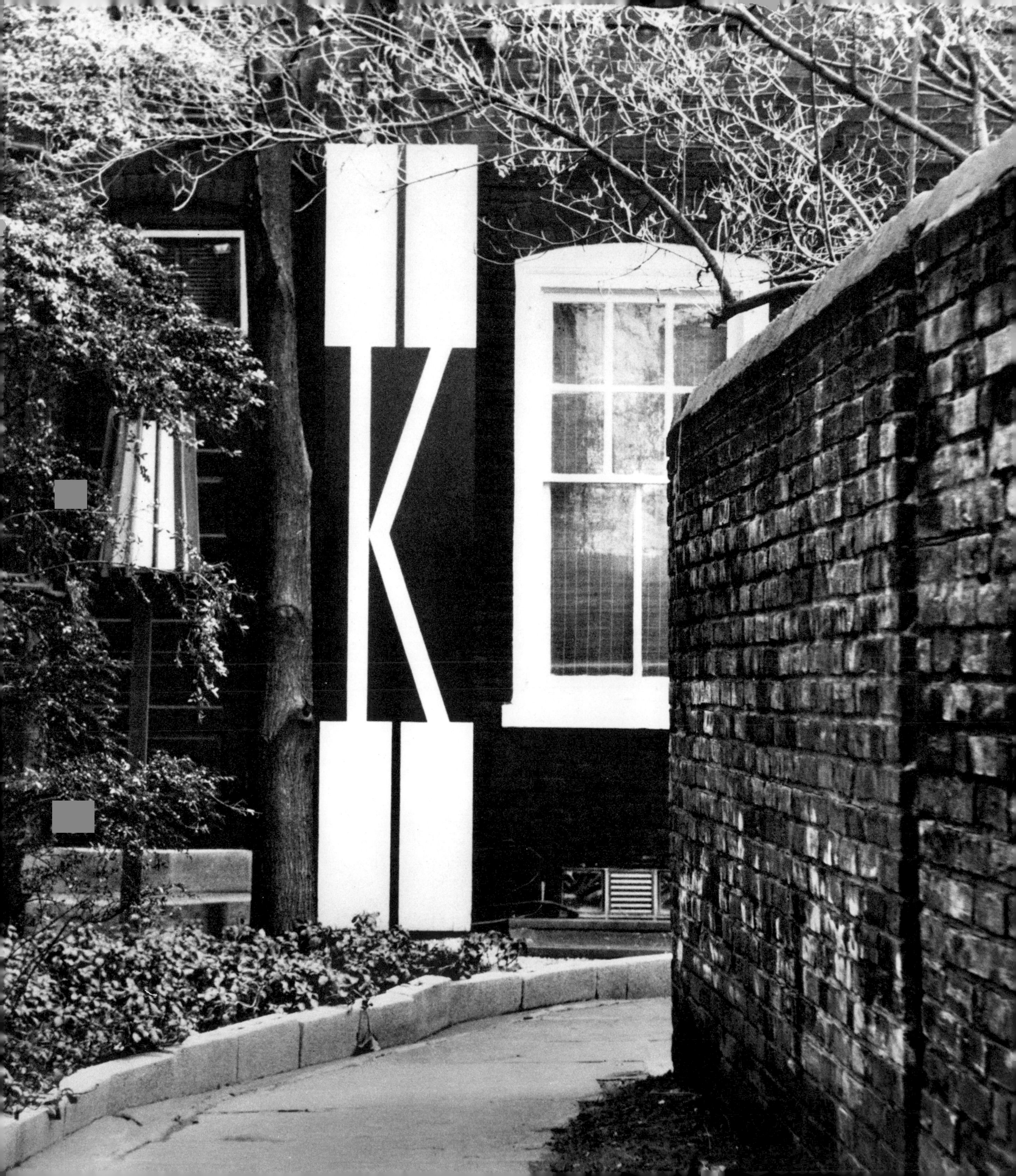
K

ITALIE
ITALY

One of the first requirements for a sign is its legibility. Despite its unusual design made from letters, this sign for a well-known toy shop in London reads easily and well.

A large panel of lettering was excellently conceived as the entrance sign to Italy's building at the Expo fair in Montreal.

MrBenson
rBensonM
BensonMr
ensonMrB
nsonMrBe
sonMrBen
onMrBens
nMrBenso
MrBenson
rBensonM
BensonMr
ensonMrB
nsonMrBe

Pride and good taste are exemplified in this combination
of numerals and letters on a panel in front of a flat in London.

The enameled numerals that have been a part of the French scene for so long are
commendable sign elements. This number makes a beautiful addition to the architecture.

This beautiful numeral in a medallion rides right out of the past on a
steam locomotive on the Aberystwyth-Devil's Bridge narrow-gauge railway in Wales.

Numerals for addresses and other purposes are often poorly done.
Nevertheless, this fine numbered medallion was found in London.

Vertical blinds, surprisingly used for a pattern of repeated letters, form the sign in a show window in London.

7 SIGNS AND ARCHITECTURE

The very word sign often suggests a separately constructed form that is placed on, near, or adjacent to a larger structure such as a building or kiosk. In some instances the signs or symbols may bear very little relationship to the general design of the larger structure.

On the other hand, there are many signs, both old and new, which are very handsomely related to the architecture. The designer has taken into consideration the lines of the building, the materials of construction, and the individual character of the structure.

Because of their height and visibility, towers of many sorts have long been used as places for clocks, sundials, weathervanes, or wind and compass direction indicators. The shop front of the English seedman's shop and the French restaurant shown in this section offer an interesting contrast. Both facades bear forms that relate to the structural whole and are also in keeping with the products to be sold. Design, abstract or natural forms, and lettering, painted or incised on the building, can be placed to explain as well as to enhance.

In many contemporary situations, the spatial restrictions of highway, street, or buildings, or prohibitive ordinances, have forced designers to use great ingenuity. As a result, signs sometimes have been placed vertically, either outside the building or upon a part of the building itself. It should be noted that in the examples shown, the whole word or name is turned vertically; the letters are not placed one above the other in oriental manner. In each instance, the vertical line of the word bears a relationship to the wall and often to the upward thrust of the building structure.

Special structures such as three-dimensional kiosks are useful where the flow of traffic goes around the form. A space-saving variety of information can be posted on a kiosk while retaining the unified form of the kiosk structure. The architectural quality of the constructed sign often bears a direct harmonious relationship to the area, the buildings, or the events. In temporary structures announcing events such as exhibitions or festivals, direct architectural contrast to the surrounding area may be desirable for easy visibility. This is especially so if the announced event is taking place in another area, not where the sign is posted.

Signs for telling time, wind direction, wind velocity, or temperature may be both functional and decorative architectural elements. This steeple with the largest clock dial in Europe is on St. Peter's Church, Zurich.

17 32.

An old sign for telling time, a sundial, is well oriented to the architecture of this Zurich building, but the clock on the church tower was found to be more dependable on a cloudy day.

The contemporary tower of the Town Hall in Hamilton, Bermuda, provides the city with information on wind direction.

W
E
N
NNW
NNE
NW
NE
WNW
ENE
W
E
WSW
ESE
SW
SE
SSW
S
SSE

LADIES HAIR STYLING
REGENCY SALON
WARDS THE SEEDSMEN.
THRIVE
TUDOR

Full advantage was taken of the relationships of carved lettering and stonework, which resulted in unified decor for this restaurant front in France.

It is to be hoped that the proprietors of this shop will resist any temptation to "go mod"; the genuine old-fashioned atmosphere of the storefront and the letters harmonize perfectly with this seedman's shop in Bath, England.

In some cities in Europe, brightly painted shutters are the symbol for an establishment selling paints. Here, the shutters act, in effect, as signs to attract attention to the shop. The script lettering over the window is commendable, as is much script lettering in Amsterdam.

The Swiss talent for decorating whole walls is shown in this example in which contemporary signs are related to the material about Goethe on the plaques higher up; this historic building is in Zurich.

IN DIESEM HAUSE
HERZOG KARL AUGUST
VON WEIMAR BEI
ST. PETERS
HOFSTATT
5
WEINSTUBE ZUR
GROSSEN REBLAUBE
H. KAISER.
WARUM STEHEN SIE DAVOR?
IST NICHT TÜRE DA UND TOR?
KÄMEN SIE GETROST HEREIN
WÜRDEN WOHL EMPFANGEN SEIN
Kaiser's Reblaube

THE BRITISH TRAVEL AND HOLIDAYS ASSOCIATION
TOURIST INFORMATION CENTRE
YORK
YORK
York is famous for its medieval walls which circle the city; and for its beautiful minster with its wealth of 13th century stained glass. York's narrow, quaint and winding streets and the richness of its historical associations make it unique among Britain's great cities.

The postings and signs for St. Raphael products in France are so colourful and decorative that they add interest to the scene in the country as well as the city. The motifs of these postings are used in many ways (see usage on a kiosk in Paris on page 164).

An interesting mural and a posting board, which add a decorative note to the street, attract attention to the entrance to the British Travel and Holidays Association center in London.

Designed to resemble a cartouche made of paper, this metal sign graces the exterior wall of a gallery in Basel, Switzerland.

Opposite in conception to the Basel sign above, this contemporary sign on a wall in Seattle uses, in a modern way, totemic symbolism of the American Northwest.

Letters incised in a plaster canopy create a decorative element on an otherwise uninteresting surface in London.

IND COOPE

Letters running vertically, reading up from bottom to top, can be used successfully where space limitations require. They add decorative interest to this shop front in New York City.

In another excellent example of the use of vertical letters, undecorated but brightly colored banners give an air of something special happening in this scene in New York City.

The Museum of Modern Art

VENEZ ELA
20

Letters used vertically relate well to letter forms used horizontally on this ticket booth at Expo in Montreal.

Vertical lettering was not necessary on this building but it lent individuality to an otherwise simple structure at Expo in Montreal.

BUKO
SMELTEOST
30%
smøre-
ost
100g
To' BUKO
til bords...
Hvorfor ikke
få Deres ege
med et
OPSPARINGSLA
HANDELSBANK
VÆR
MED
NU!
UNGDOMMENS
TEATER
europa danser
i K.B. hallen
europa danser
i K.B. hallen
europa danser
i K.B. hallen
europa danser
i K.B. hallen
europa danser
i K.B. hallen
TIVOLI
Varieteen
INTERNATIONAL
SHOW
MUSIC
HALL
PREBEN
UGLEBJERG
SENOR WENCES
PEIRO BROTHERS
KAZBEK & ZARI
TIVOLI

A section of a building that might be considered a kiosk is
used here for the dispensing of tobacco products in Coventry, England.

Kiosks in the street are familiar architectural elements in many cities, and serve
many useful purposes including the posting of signs. The kiosk on the far left is in Paris.
Round kiosks are used for displaying posters and other signs, making
the Copenhagen street scene illustrated at the left visually exciting.

JOHN ESHER LTD.
HEAD HOUSE
TAVERN

This is another good example of a display structure that relates very well to the surrounding architecture; Smithville, New Jersey.

Information can be given in an interesting way when signs are designed as street structures. This triangular sign, illuminated from its interior, is handsome in itself, and relates well to the architecture of an eighteenth-century restoration shopping area in Philadelphia.

A sign structure in contemporary styling was used to attract attention to a gardening exhibition in 1959 in Zurich.

A contemporary structure for clocks was well related to the surrounding architectural scene at Expo, Montreal.

Heure Officielle
Official Time

8 TRAVEL AND DIRECTION

With the population increase in the last century came an increase in the means of travel and movement, and with it the need for a greater number of signs and symbols. Inn signs with details best observed at a leisurely pace, or signs that listed a multitude of names or information, do not now suffice. The message must be visual, direct, and easily remembered so that immediate action can be taken. The symbol has come into even greater use today in the form of arrows, one- or two-way indicators, circles, and silhouettes of things such as trucks, children, and construction sites.

The average pedestrian needs, literally, to watch his step. He may see the traffic light ahead but at his feet there may also be an abstract form of a path or a pattern of stripes indicating a general pedestrian crossing. There may also be arrows leading to a safety zone, or lines indicating where he may not cross, as well as indications of where vehicles must stop for his convenience or safety.

The motorist, too, needs to interpret at a glance a turn-off sign on a large highway, the curve ahead, or the parking area. Signs along an expressway need to be interpreted at a glance from a speeding vehicle, for immediate action. Therefore, the letter forms must be simple and legible, lanes clearly marked, and symbols for traffic changes easily identifiable. Signs on moving vehicles such as trucks, trains, or airplanes must be designed to communicate the company name and product at a glance, in a way that can be remembered in the future.

Corporate images must include the corporations' signs, as well as the design of their vehicles, and the total design images must relate to the services offered. It is interesting to note that signs for traffic flow and control are very similarly designed and used in many countries; the most effective ones are usually the simplest and the most graphically pleasing. In one illustration in this section a warning sign uses simplified pictorial humor without a single word to communicate a very memorable message.

In most European cities pedestrians have the right of way when walking on crosswalks, marked by stripes painted underfoot. Vehicular traffic must stop when pedestrians approach these boldly marked areas.

A simple, well-conceived sign set underfoot creates a bit of needed visual interest in the drabness of so many streets and sidewalks.

The signs shown here are set in the street in tile; the one at the left is in Amsterdam and the one above in Venice, Italy.

Certainly this is a strategic position for pedestrian observation of street signs, but one wonders what happens to these signs posted on the curbside in Milan, Italy, on and after a rainy, muddy day.

With the density and speed of much vehicular traffic, easily seen symbols on streets and highways are not only practical but necessary.

C.R.SMITH & SON
10 11 12 1 2 3 4 5 6 7 8 9

This old plate embedded in the pavement was useful for traffic that moved no faster than the speed of a horse and carriage. Embedded signs are still useful in congested areas, or where street identification is confusingly placed or turned by pranksters or accidents.

Identification is one of the many functions of signs. "Sack" made sure of perpetuating his identity by taking advantage of the softness of new cement.

This brass sign, set in cement, has been in a Philadelphia street for many years. Despite heavy pedestrian traffic, the sign is in excellent condition.

PRINCE OF WALES
BRITISH
RAILWAYS

Very simple purposes often create surprisingly unusual compositions of forms and letters; these were photographed on a freight car in Sweden.

Vehicles for public transportation, particularly steam locomotives, have a long history of good signs and letters; these are on the sides of a locomotive of the Aberystwyth-Devil's Bridge narrow-gauge railway in Wales.

Deliberate, simple, straightforward, and informative is this excellent traffic control sign in Stockholm.

There is no doubt that excellence and quality goods are suggested by silver letters on a florist's delivery truck in Philadelphia.

Trademark letters are effectively applied to the small delivery trucks of a store in Stockholm.

A good example of visual graphics shown on a small delivery truck.

Organizations large and small should appreciate the identification value of well-planned symbolism. Here is a strikingly successful example of the application of a contemporary corporate symbol to vehicles.

When license plates are exploited as advertisements, for states, nations, or territories, their readability is lessened. The identification plates for British vehicles are examples of simple, efficient signs.

Identification of aircraft has a tradition going back to World War I fighter planes; the simple and effective jet aircraft symbols shown here are for Continental and Texas International Airlines.

N32717

Even equipment that travels vertically can be useful for identification purposes; London.

Unusually attractive because the large circular elements were constantly revolving, this large sign presented the theme of Expo in Montreal. At one moment in the revolution, it becomes, graphically, as shown in the bottom photograph, "The Symbol of Man."

Le Symbole de l'Homme
The Symbol of Man

Le Symbole de l'Homme
The Symbol of Man

This mileage marker has little practical virtue in a fast-moving, contemporary world. It has survived in a country that treasures fine things of other periods and is a bit of nostalgia still standing beside a British highway.

Contrasting sharply with the sign above, this highway marker is typical of Britain's fine solutions to contemporary traffic sign problems.

These ingenious signs in Amsterdam serve two purposes: telling the bicyclist where to park, and providing a simple means of doing so.

A graphic, lucid sign in Chartres, France.

à 100 mètres
sens
giratoire
659
BQ·28

These illustrations show effective traffic control signs without words. The one on the left is at a dangerously sharp mountain curve on the Mohawk trail in Massachusetts, and the ones above are at a street corner in Amsterdam.

BIBLIOGRAPHY

Constantine, Mildred, and Jacobson, Egbert. *Sign Language.* New York: Reinhold, 1961.

Creux, René, *Old Inn Signs in Switzerland.* Lausanne. Paudex, 1962.

Creux, René. *Images dans le Ciel.* Lausanne: Editions de Fontainmore, 1962.

Etiemble. *The Orion Book of the Written Word.* New York: Orion Press, 1961.

Finsterer-Stuber, Gerda. *Marken und Signete.* Stuttgart: Julius Hoffmann Verlag, 1957.

Gombrich, E. H. *Art and Illusion.* New York: Bollingen Foundation, Pantheon Books, 1961.

Kamekura, Yusaku. *Trademarks and Symbols of the World.* New York: Van Nostrand Reinhold, 1965.

Koch, Rudolf. *The Book of Signs.* New York: Dover Publications, 1955.

Lalou, Etienne. "Le Soleil," *Encyclopédie Essentielle.* Paris: Robert Delpire, 1958.

Lehner, Ernst. *Symbols, Signs & Signets.* New York: Dover Publications, 1969.

Rosen, Ben. *The Corporate Search for Visual Identity.* New York: Van Nostrand Reinhold, 1970.

Sutton, James. *Signs in Action.* London: Studio Vista; New York: Van Nostrand Reinhold, 1965.

Wildbur, Peter. *Trademarks.* London: Studio Vista; New York: Van Nostrand Reinhold, 1966.

A convincing message without words at a ferry crossing in Wales.